Praise for
Fight

"I felt like I was reading a Tom Clancy book on spiritual warfare. An enjoyable read on a deadly serious subject. You won't be disappointed."
> —DAVID MURROW, author, *Why Men Hate Going to Church*

"*Fight* is all about a radically alternative way to fight the good fight against the forces of evil in order to finish well with victory! Kenny Luck got my adrenaline pumping. *Fight* is a 'gotta' read for every Christ warrior."
> —DR. WALT KALLESTAD, author of *Entrepreneurial Faith*, *A Passionate Life*, *The Passionate Church*, and *Turn Your Church Inside Out*, and senior pastor of Community Church of Joy in Glendale, Arizona

"It's been said that all evil needs to succeed is for good men to do nothing. Kenny excels at showing the bigger story we're engaged in. *Fight* is a must read for men to defeat the enemy where *each of us* live—in our marriages, our families, and all our spheres of influence."
> —JIM WEIDMANN, "The Family Night Guy," senior vice president of Promise Keepers, and author of the Family Night Tool Chest series

"I always want to know if the author of a book exemplifies what he has written. Kenny Luck certainly does!"
> —TOM HOLLADAY, teaching pastor at Saddleback Church and author of *Foundations: 11 Core Truths to Build Your Life On*

"As a pastor, I get the joy of seeing how Kenny's message lives out weekly through our men at Saddleback Church. It's not theory, but real! Kenny's passion and calling is making a difference!"
> —DOUG SLAYBAUGH, president, Purpose Driven

fight

fight

Are you willing to pick a
Fight with Evil?

kenny luck

WATERBROOK
PRESS

FIGHT
PUBLISHED BY WATERBROOK PRESS
12265 Oracle Boulevard, Suite 200
Colorado Springs, Colorado 80921
A division of Random House Inc.

Italics in Scripture quotations indicate the author's added emphasis.

Details in some anecdotes and stories have been changed to protect the identities of the persons involved.

ISBN 978-1-57856-988-5

Published in the United States by WaterBrook Multnomah, an imprint of The Doubleday Publishing Group, a division of Random House Inc., New York.

Library of Congress Cataloging-in-Publication Data
Luck, Kenneth L., 1964–
    Fight : are you willing to pick a fight with evil? / Kenny Luck.
        p. cm.
    ISBN 978-1-57856-988-5
  1. Spiritual warfare. 2. Good and evil. I. Title.
    BV4509.5.L83 2008
    248.8'42—dc22

                                        2008003714

Printed in the United States of America
2008—First Edition

10 9 8 7 6 5 4 3 2 1

To God's men…
"in order that Satan might not outwit us.
For we are not unaware of his schemes."
2 Corinthians 2:11

contents

Part 1: Facing Evil

Part 2: Discerning Evil

Part 3: Engaging Evil

part 1

facing evil

chapter 1

ignorance is incompetence

It is a very human and natural response to fear the unknown.
For a believer to keep himself in the dark about Satan's person
and work is a dangerous mistake.

—MARK BUBECK

I don't know of any book that actually *invites* you to begin picking more
fights with evil.

And yet you're holding it.

Aside from what that says about you, I'm well aware that holding this
book may cause some men to feel like Hal, the deer from *The Far Side*
comic with the bull's-eye birthmark on his chest. Fact is, you and Hal
do have this birthmark issue in common. You've been marked and labeled
in the spiritual world just by virtue of your birth. If you claim the family
name of Christian, you are being hunted to be destroyed.

And yet a lot of us are denying this dance to the death even exists. We've heard of the battle and may even be aware of it to some extent, but it's all to little practical effect. We've been duped and made to forget that, unlike Gary Larson's deer, the hunted God's man can actually turn the tables on evil and become the hunter. We have the power and ability to send the hunter packing! It's all a matter of perceiving the spiritual reality and understanding the source of authority.

Most believers are aware of the "right answers" when it comes to the familiar idea of waging spiritual warfare. And yet we're failing at practical application. We look at the cosmic conflict between good and evil more like a Harry Potter movie—it's a tossup as to which side will prevail until the final frame. And it's this perspective when applied to the *real world* of spiritual attack that breeds insecurity, hesitation, vacillation, and harm to both believer and the cause of Christ.

I, for one, am loath to take on *that* reputation. I trust you're with me.

No Interest or Just No Stomach?

We will have struck a deep blow to our enemy if our concept of the spiritual battle moves forcefully from being an afterthought to a way to believe and behave. Based on the attitudes I encounter in men world-wide regarding evil, *I would want us for an opponent if I were Satan.* The painful, sad reality is that the underworld has the upper hand on the ground level of this war with God's men. I'll address this later in the book in detail, but for now let's just say we've been assuming the submissive position of a scared pooch, or been freely giving permission (by our inaction) to evil to trample over our lives and the world with impunity. A reality check is in order.

It's time to look in the mirror and not be satisfied with what we have become in the midst of the great war for our King. We must make peace with the fact that we are spiritually enabled, empowered, and equipped to make war on the Enemy and *do something*. We are commissioned to inflict losses, unmask and thwart plots to kill, and deliver those in bondage to darkness into the freedom of the sons of light.

Satan knows who you are. Get that. Then, as every God's man must do on a more urgent basis, you need to accept what that means. What's *that,* you say? Simple: You cannot ask for a hall pass to get out of this fight. You must also stop living in ignorance and denial. Instead, you need to understand and get to know Satan's ways. Why? Because you are in play à la Jason Bourne. You are an asset on assignment to neutralize evil wherever and whenever it rears its insidious head. You are to be feared by the Enemy, not laughed at.

> *Satan knows who you are. Get that. Then, as every God's man must do on a more urgent basis, you need to accept what that means.*

When I signed on to write the God's Man series, there was a deep sense of foreboding every time I pondered the third book (this one). I was, all at once, deeply convicted and committed to stimulating more intelligent and intentional kingdom warfare *and* intensely aware of what I would be asking for—troubles of another kind. Devilishly bizarre dreams, personal attacks, marital roadside bombs, harassing thoughts, family traumas, conflicts with church members, a double root canal, and a tsunami of satanic diversions are just a sampling of the mortar and artillery rounds that have been lobbed my way. While some of these are just natural events, the negative emotions that come with them are what the Devil loves to cultivate and exploit in a believer. Every excuse to discourage me, Satan took. He doesn't play fair and is the king of low blows. He waits to kick men in the teeth when they're down. Magnifying emotions to create insecurities, heighten fears, and defeat us without a bullet being shot are the things Satan is best at. He must rely on playing mind games—a sign of insecurity and no real power. Nonetheless, he's allowed to mess with us.

He is doing the same thing with you *right now.*

Repeatedly the message from Satan was, "I know who you are and what you intend to do." A little preemptive retaliation is consistent warfare doctrine among sovereigns who feel that the security of their networks or borders is *about to be compromised in some way.* These shots across the bow were intended to say, "Do you really want this? You might want to reconsider." Throughout this time God's Spirit has said, "Reconsider this!" like we read in the fourth chapter of Luke's Gospel when Jesus quit listening and started rebuking evil suggestions and ploys. Well, my friend, I am still here dialoguing with you on these pages, and Satan still knows where I live. Boo-ya!

I wanted you to know a little thunder has been rolling my way, but I expected this. I knew all hell would break loose before, during, and after my decision to focus an entire manuscript on outing the Devil and equipping you to effectively confront and defeat him. I knew the Devil loathes being discovered the way any terrorist would be incensed at the man who blew his cover. I knew that the Great Pimp has a big ego matched only by that noxious chip on his shoulder toward believers. I knew that anyone who actively pulls his masks off to expose his presence is asking for a double helping of ire and indignation.

And yet many days what kept me going was *you.* Yes, you—the God's man reading these words. The reason you have this book in your hands is because *you* have been called by your King for this hour. You are being asked to join the company of other mighty men to be the tip of the spear in the war against evil. Just the word *fight* resonated with your soul and spirit. You are cognizant of the smell of war in your own life, and you see it in your world. *That* willingness to fight is being affirmed by God's Spirit. Your training as a disciple is ready to go the next level. *Your* strong, confident, and fully surrendered presence is going to be needed. Your quickening to the battle is at hand.

I know this feeling well.

Writing *Fight* was unnerving *and* necessary for me. Reading *Fight* will be the same for you. The realities and truths you will confront in these pages will both unnerve you and compel a necessary faith response. More bluntly, from this time forward you will need to change the way you address the challenges of life to account for evil and its presence in and around you. In effect, you are being handed a pair of night-vision goggles (another topic we'll take on later), and you will see "movement" of evil that was previously hidden. You will feel the apprehension one experiences when he is considering war. Satan wants you to feel the fear. God will replace that fear with Himself.

These are how all rites of passage feel to a surrendered God's man. God's men are filled with spiritual tension because something is actually at stake. There is the tension you feel when your faith collides with the reality of your responsibility to it. *Risk* dealt with this. Then there is the tension of becoming the man you were created to be versus the man you thought you ought to be. *Dream* addressed this issue in your life. Then there is the rite of passage most men do not have the stomach to address: facing the reality and tension of dealing directly with evil. *Fight* will stretch you again and again to *see, engage, face, call out,* and *demolish* evil with confidence and skill *through* Christ. So men wearing spiritual skirts need not apply. Jesus didn't own one, and as His representative possessing His authority, neither should you. "The reason the Son of God appeared was to destroy the devil's work" (1 John 3:8). Take heart, you have an excellent Mentor.

But let's stow the macho talk for a second and get down to the sweat and blood of what's to come.

Your Attitude and Your Stand

Your attitude about evil reflects your stand against evil.

The great men of faith understood this, and as God's man, so must you. To help you with this, we need to think about evil and our fight with it in uncomplicated terms that are consistent with Scripture and practical to apply. We need to think better before we can fight better. The "We've got Jesus, yes we do. We've got Jesus, how about you?" approach is as effective as it sounds. The Bible does not support it, though it might work at Vacation Bible School. In fact, the more emotional you are in warfare, the sooner you die. So in the interest of living to fight another day, let's replace emotional and unsuccessful strategies with intelligent and intentional ways of thinking about and fighting evil. For starters, let's wipe the board clean of what we think we know about evil and resolve to stick to Scripture's direction and plan for how we are going to prepare for the fight.

On the whiteboard in my office you will see this written at the top: INFORMATION WITHOUT APPLICATION IS HALLUCINATION. As in the other books in this series (*Risk* and *Dream*), the overriding objective is real-time application of spiritual truth. That means it's time to embrace these five *Fight* principles in order to change your attitude and, consequently, your personal stand against the evil powers of this present age. You will be pushed, in increasing ways, to

Face the Reality of Evil

Integrate Intel on the Enemy

Grow Progressively More Aware of Evil

Handle Your Weapons with Consistency and Confidence

Take the Fight to Evil

These are the core tactics connected to owning the night and not letting evil hide under the cover of deceptive masks.

1. Face the Reality of Evil

There was a time before September 11, 2001, when counterterrorist agencies possessed good intelligence about a group called Al-Qaida. We knew who their leader was and where he was, we knew where their training facilities were, we knew how to "touch" them, and we knew the United States was the object of their Islamofascist brand of hatred. And yet, with so many other higher-priority issues, international and domestic crises, and lack of "actionable intelligence," we didn't assign enough attention to this character Osama bin Laden and his terrorist network. The world knows the rest of the story.

Granted, foresight is always 20/40, or worse. You can see some things, but not much of it clearly. You can discern a good portion of the picture, but the small details and facts are a little fuzzy. Hindsight, on the other hand, is *always* 20/20, or better. The pain or trauma acts like window cleaner. We learn from our mistakes; we evaluate and assess what went wrong. Between foresight and hindsight is a crucial lesson in the battle with evil: *when all you have is fuzzy foresight, you must focus more attention and resources on the Enemy who wants your head on a platter.* If you do, your hindsight will be much less painful.

Of all the lessons America learned from the 9/11 terrorist attack, the biggie was that we simply did not connect the threats with the reality of such a large-scale operation on our own soil. We believed the terrorists were out there, but we acted like we "sort of" believed the intel. Sort of believing in a real enemy and real threat produces a sort-of response that sort of gets people killed. We no longer sort of believe in terrorists who want to kill us. We have been baptized by fire into a new reality regarding the lethal intentions, scope, and scale of global terrorism.

> *Sort of believing in a real enemy and real threat produces a sort-of response that sort of gets people killed.*

Satan unequivocally wants you dead or at least neutralized (living but not a threat). For God's man the most tragic mistake you can make is to sort of believe in evil, its existence, and its specific designs on your life. When God's men approach the reality of evil this way, we send a clear message to our enemy. What we are saying is that intellectually and mentally we believe there is an evil ringleader guiding plots against us, but practically, we act as though he has nothing to do with what befalls us. We behave like all our problems have natural causes and solutions; none have supernatural causes and divine solutions. We end up responding to problems that require supernatural responses with human wisdom and natural solutions. We are firing water pistols at an armed destroyer.

While we may not be disbelievers in evil or overbelievers (where the Devil is behind everything bad that happens), functionally we are sort-of believers, and God's men are getting killed. The casualties among even our best fighting men tell the whole story. Blood is being spilled. Because we do not account for evil in the right way, it has its way in our lives and in the world. Low-priority status on evil creates a dysfunctional and fatal vulnerability. Jesus never taught His men this. He spoke openly of how the Thief, Killer, and Destroyer would actively oppose Him in the present. In fact, Jesus directly said that God's people would live side by side with evil forces and people until He returned.

> The kingdom of heaven is like a man who sowed good seed in his field. But while everyone was sleeping, his enemy came and sowed weeds among the wheat, and went away. When the wheat sprouted and formed heads, then the weeds also appeared.
>
> The owner's servants came to him and said, "Sir, didn't you sow good seed in your field? Where then did the weeds come from?"
>
> "An enemy did this," he replied.
>
> The servants asked him, "Do you want us to go and pull them up?"
>
> "No," he answered, "because while you are pulling the weeds, you may root up the wheat with them. Let both grow together until the harvest. At that time I will tell the harvesters: First collect the weeds and tie them in bundles to be burned; then gather the wheat and bring it into my barn." (Matthew 13:24–30)

The owner's servants acted surprised to see those evil weeds among the good wheat. The looks on their faces said, "That is not supposed to be here." Their expectations were off. The wheat plants (us) are going to have to contend for survival among the weeds (evil). For those who deny the side-by-side existence of evil with man in this present age, Jesus' words will not encourage you. However, they might help you embrace the first key principle: facing and embracing the reality that evil doesn't just appear now and then when bad things happen, *it is all around you.* The good seed are the sons of the kingdom. The bad seed are the sons of the Evil One. The field is the world. In this "not yet" time between eternities, there is no separation of God's people from evil; it's a mixed bag. There is no escaping it. So how are we supposed to live as God's men during this "not yet time" with a clear and present evil among us? At a minimum, we need to act more consistently with reality. That's God's position.

Face it: Satan has been watching film on you. He's relentless. Get that one firmly planted in your brain. Even *after* getting taken to the shed by the Son of God, the Bible says that "he left him *until the next opportunity came*" (Luke 4:13, NLT 2004). Satan is not just relentless but a relentless opportunist. He *never* rests. This is the big pink elephant parked in the middle of the church today, and there are only two options in dealing with it: live in reality or live in fantasy. One attitude is very comfortable, and the other is uncomfortable. But when it comes to being God's man, discipleship and discomfort are very closely connected.

Being with Jesus in the first century meant regular discussions about Satan and engaging evil forces. Imagine: for the disciples, being with Jesus was for the specific intention of gaining the authority and training to cast out demons! The Gospels, the book of Acts, the pastoral epistles, and John's vision in Revelation all talk about evil making its play in the life of the believers. The norm for a New Testament God's man is to regularly recognize and deal with evil.

Today this kind of fearlessness is completely absent. Spiritual warfare is considered too "out there," misinformation, or someone else's calling.

The Bible calls Satan "the ruler of this world." Thinking wrongly about him, or not at all, gives him his greatest tactical advantage.

Hitler said, "What luck for rulers that men do not think." Where do you think *that* thought came from? It's time to snap out of it.

2. Integrate Intel of the Enemy

My friend Bill (not his real name) works in a counterterrorism center. Here's the stated mission of his team in their handbook:

> To integrate…threat intelligence and provide for intake, analysis, fusion, synthesis, and dissemination of that information…. The center converts the information into operational intelligence to detect, deter, and defend against terrorist attacks…within the seven counties assigned to this unit.[1]

Bill's whole job is to integrate, analyze, and synthesize threat intelligence so that he can identify patterns, trends, and what he calls "potentials," which might indicate an emerging threat. When Bill gets a "hit" and the information coalesces into an emerging threat, he supplies the relevant and actionable intelligence to prepare a preemptive response to the threat.

The next time you hear about the threat level being raised to Orange or Red by Homeland Security, think about the men and women like Bill who focus solely on sifting through complicated and convoluted data to get a threat picture. Then think about having the personal courage to act on that data without hesitation or trepidation. This is what a counterterrorism agent is trained to do. They are good at putting together the pieces of suspicious activity related to terrorist plots.

God's man and Bill have this is common: both are tasked with integrating intelligence on terrorist threats. Then they must have the courage to sound the alarm and put a preemptive response in motion. Intelligence provides the clues and smells they need.

In fact, in helping the Corinthians, the apostle Paul acted just like the spiritual counterterrorism expert we are describing. As he gathered information about all the conflicts among believers over various issues, he saw an emerging pattern and trend as he analyzed the data. Lo and behold, the fingerprints of the Evil One were popping up in his mental database. Finally, after various roadside bombs had gone off in Corinth with the intent to divide and destabilize believers, Paul integrated and then acted on that analysis to combat the terrorist threat against the body like a true terrorism liaison officer (TLO). He supplied actionable intelligence for the believers.

> The reason I wrote you was to see if you would stand the test and be obedient in everything. If you forgive anyone, I also forgive him. And what I have forgiven—if there was anything to forgive—I have forgiven in the sight of Christ for your sake, *in order that Satan might not outwit us. For we are not unaware of his schemes.* (2 Corinthians 2:9–11)

Translation: Based on the intel, we know who's *really* behind this and we're going to take the necessary steps (join in forgiving people) to stop this terrorist threat. The sledgehammer application is this: If you are *unaware,* you will be *outwitted* by evil. If you are outwitted, people around you get hurt, and the cause of the kingdom suffers. The reverse scenario is equally valid. If you are actively integrating your intelligence and matrixing that intel with what you know to be true about how evil operates, you will preempt and shut down the Devil's terrorist schemes against you, other believers, the church, and the world. Here's the scary part: we have the actionable intel straight from Jesus Himself, the terrorist playbook exposed in the Word of God, and the Holy Spirit available to help discern and coordinate the tactical pieces. And yet we are unwilling and/or failing to integrate these resources in order to take preemptive action against the Great Terrorist and his schemes.

God's man is duty bound to integrate the intel God has provided. Versus what? Neglecting, dismissing, or being ambivalent about it. God hasn't provided Satan's file to us for nothing. We need to learn everything we can about him and his methods of operation. Then we need to raise our threat level to Red and keep it there.

3. Grow Progressively More Aware of Evil

Predators thrive on their prey being unaware of their presence. Spiders spin translucent webs. Sharks have sensors running the length of their bodies that detect an unsuspecting "lunch" before the lunch detects the shark. Alligators and crocodiles rely on stealth and stillness while their prey unwittingly walks into their viselike jaws. Birds of prey fall out of the sky with talons fanned out and ready to clench. In all these cases, the victims do not see their end coming.

Other times in nature you see the exact opposite. Birds spot predators and call out a warning. Monkey or baboon troops have a sentry network and give the universal "get outta here, predator is in the house" yell that activates the flight response of the group. Other animals use their sense of smell, sonar, visual awareness, or other God-engineered warning systems to avoid an untimely end. Most animals know whose menu they're on, who represents a threat, and when things aren't right—hopefully in time

> ## fight fact
> *Just as unaware and unproductive go hand in hand, awareness of evil is synonymous with effectiveness against evil. In war, intel goes before bullets or bombs.*

to act. When you are a potential meal at any moment, let's just say you develop a little sensitivity to certain characters and factors occurring in your environment.

The wild-kingdom metaphor is one God thought we should learn from. God's man needs to grow an aggressive awareness of evil and its opportunistic method of eating believers alive. "Keep a cool head. Stay alert. The Devil is poised to pounce, and would like nothing better than to catch you napping. Keep your guard up" (1 Peter 5:8–9, MSG). Heady. Alert. Guard up. Any other attitude toward the active and present threat of evil is, by default, suicidal. This might be termed an aggressive awareness based on the recognition of reality. When you are not awake and aware, you are asleep and vulnerable. A reactive strategy usually means you're too late. Too late means you find fangs in the back of your neck. This style of spiritual living might be

> *"The history of failure in war can almost be summed up in two words, too late."*

labeled an indifferent laziness rooted in ignorance or apathy or both. An unaware, unprepared God's man is a biblical oxymoron. Key word: moron.

Bend over a watering hole in front of a salivating lion and watch what happens.

Gen. Douglas MacArthur had a propensity for noting the obvious when it came to fighting wars, winning battles, and avoiding defeats. D. Mac's wisdom is telling for every God's man. "The history of failure in war can almost be summed up in two words, too late. Too late in comprehending the deadly purpose of a potential enemy. Too late in realizing mortal danger. Too late in preparedness. Too late in uniting all possible forces for resistance. Too late in standing with one's friends."[2]

It's not too late…yet.

4. Handle Your Weapons with Consistency and Confidence

Ever gone paintballing? Here's some advice: don't go with a marine.

My friend Paul is a retired Devil Dog and marine F-18 pilot. For Paul's fortieth birthday his wife paid for a group of us to kidnap and transport him down to his old stomping grounds at Camp Pendleton for some war games with his buddies. *Games* is a bad word for what transpired. *Duck shoot* would be more accurate—especially for the birthday boy. No man relishes the sheer enjoyment of peppering your backside with colored buckshot more than Paul. Quite a few of us were the privileged targets of his experienced marksmanship. When technical expertise is married with tactical awareness in one man, *don't* hand him an air rifle that fires a projectile five hundred fifty feet per second! Or at least make sure he is on *your* team. You get hit in your privates, don't know where he is, and then hear him laughing at you! At the end of the day we had a welt pageant courtesy of the shooter. Here is another Fight Fact:

A nation can purchase the most technically advanced weapons on the planet, but if its soldiers do not realize those weapons' capabilities, they have wasted millions and hurt their cause.

fight fact
Training with weapons breeds accuracy with weapons. The untrained will always pay a price.

That basic law of warfare holds true for God's man and the arsenal of weapons God has provided for him to combat and defeat evil. Modern spiritual warfare is no different from the old-fashioned kind, because the eternal and spiritual weapons we use against evil do not change. Spiritual weapons do not evolve to match the battlefield conditions. A man's *resolve* to be intimate with them and use them skillfully does *evolve* and determines victory or defeat.

Jesus is our ultimate trainer in the art of spiritual battle. His weapons are our weapons, passed through the ages to men of faith. The goal is to handle them skillfully. Versus what? Versus clumsily and incompetently. In our hearts we know confidently understanding our arsenal will mean a confident mentality and stance under fire. With a real, supernatural showdown looming with a highly trained enemy, only arrogance and stupidity would cause a God's man to reach for self-prescribed wisdom and solutions. "We are human, but we don't wage war with human plans and methods. We use God's mighty weapons, not mere worldly weapons, to knock down the Devil's strongholds" (2 Corinthians 10:3–4, NLT 1996).

The weapons God has supplied are to be *used* against evil. Not just used before meals, when calamities strike, or to make your life more comfortable and pain free. Mighty weapons need to be placed into the proper hands because, *properly handled,* they pack quite a punch. You don't hand firearms to children or immature novices. They don't know what they are holding, and they underappreciate the danger. That makes me pause. God's man appreciates the danger, is intimate with his weapons, and knows why he possesses them: to resist, rebuke, repel, and vanquish evil with righteous intent.

Only use and familiarity make you dangerous with a weapon.

5. Take the Fight to Evil

Reality demands responses, and some things need to be said now about choosing this fight. The days of being emotionally distant and ambivalent toward evil are over. With knowledge comes responsibility, and with responsibility comes some new choices that will uncover our commitment to fight or renew our willingness to fight harder and longer. My brother, the facts go like this: You are about to embark on the greatest crusade known to men and angels. Heaven is watching, and the hopes and prayers of your brothers march with you. Locking arms with other brave soldiers in Christ serving on other fronts, you will be called to bring about the destruction of evil plots against the good, the elimination of the stranglehold of Satan over the lives of others, and the advancement of the kingdom of God.

This undertaking will not be trouble free or painless. Your enemy is intelligent, skilled, and personally driven by his cause. He will fight viciously. But God's Spirit declares this is a new day for men He is making new. The tide is turning, and the days of living in defeat and despair have been replaced with the full commitment of God's men who are willing to fight in the open, hand to hand. Our collective focus on exposing, isolating, and moving aggressively against evil will change and reduce evil's capacity to wage war. We have overwhelmingly superior weaponry placed at our disposal and rising numbers of skilled warriors locking arms. God's men are on the march, and we are resolved to accept nothing less than a full victory, even if that means our very lives.

God has full confidence in your loyalty to His cause and your abilities to fight for Him when you are called upon by circumstances and the commission of Christ. Your King has declared to you, *"All authority in heaven and on earth has been given to* me" (Matthew 28:18). It's time we get that and deal with evil the right way—expose it, engage it, and keep it on the run *through* Christ.

To become God's man, you will

Face the reality of evil head on

Integrate the intelligence God has provided in Scripture

Grow progressively more aware of Satan's presence

Handle your weapons with skill and dangerous intention

Take the fight to the Enemy

As you read, watch for the image of the fighter's hands. When you see the hands, remember, it's a place of application. That's your signal to stop, pause, examine yourself, and reflect on a spiritual principle. In the chapters ahead you will find that the biggest battle you will fight with the Enemy is in your own head. Discipline your mind, because the attacks upon it will increase. The true spirit of fighting as God's man is allowing yourself to be directed by God and applying what He shows you. Every application will require your surrender in order to secure your victories. Ready yourself.

A new thunder is coming.

the nonfiction demon

It is significant testimony to the reality of demons that every
writer of the New Testament, except the author of Hebrews,
mentions demons or evil angels. Even Hebrews, however,
directly names the devil (Hebrews 2:14).

—C. Fred Dickason

"Kenny, I need you to fast and pray before coming in to work tomorrow."

A cold chill ran up my spine as I took in Darren's eyes and what he'd just
said. No "Hello, how's it going?" or "Hey, want to grab some lunch?"
The urgency stunned me.

In almost any context, the request might bring to mind one of those
everyday but still unique circumstances that require extra attention. You
know, maybe a surgery for a loved one or a career decision. But on a
locked unit in a psychiatric hospital, such urgency is another story. My
brain worked at warp speed to discern what that other story could be and
in nanoseconds put it all together. There are only a few contexts biblically

and practically where a request like this might be put out there brother to brother. I thought about it. "This kind does not go out except by prayer and fasting" (Matthew 17:21, NASB). *BING! BING! BING!* I knew that was it. We were going to have a power encounter with evil with one of our patients on the locked unit. I knew without Darren even explaining.

I'd been waiting for those ominous words from one of our chaplains for many years. As a director of inpatient psychiatric programs, I had a lot of direct contact with patients: bipolar disorders, manic depression, psychosis, schizophrenia, suicidality, homicidality, eating disorders, self-mutilating compulsions, religious delusion, and dual-diagnosis maladies of the mind and body (people who medicate psychological and psychiatric diagnoses with chemical substances). On top of this, my own immediate family had experienced psychotic episodes we'd had to manage carefully and delicately, with the best interventions available. All of those occurred, to the best of my knowledge, without demonic causes.

Certainly, the delusional and psychotic side of psychiatric health care was always a wild ride and required a certain acceptance of strangeness. In many instances patients believed they were historical characters. Just for starters, I had personally encountered Jesus, Mary, the apostle Paul, and Barnabas. On one occasion one of our "apostles" secretly took other patients to the Jacuzzi to baptize them as part of a delusional episode. Mental health work is no laughing matter, but occasionally you've just got to laugh, maybe to keep from crying. For many families, including my own, the term *living hell* is not far from the truth.

So…by now you're probably saying, "Enough of the diagnostic world of mental health!" But here's the thing. It's important for you to know a little about my background because there are many Christians and so-called experts who wouldn't be able to tell the difference between a true demon invasion and mental illness. Many people suffering from psychologically and chemically induced pathology have been misdiagnosed by well-intentioned Christians as demonized, and certain people who have manifested demonic pathology have been misdiagnosed and mistreated by mental health professionals.

I have seen both sides.

Then add Darren. He was a credentialed, clinical pastoral chaplain, and he spent years as a missionary in Zaire (the

> *His request to fast and pray before coming to work was loud and clear. Someone was struggling against evil and needed help.*

Democratic Republic of the Congo today) where he came face to face with demonic inhabitation on a regular basis. To boot, he received his master's of divinity from Fuller Seminary, one of the best seminaries in the country. So the man speaking these words to me was not some two-bit TV preacher using choreographed scare tactics. The look in his eyes conveyed a humble confidence born of experience; his posture and demeanor were those of a spiritual warrior. In this context, his request to fast and pray before coming to work was loud and clear. Someone was struggling against evil and needed help. And he was asking me to be his wing man in the battle.

That got my adrenaline flowing.

Darren had become aware something else was going on with the woman in room 302, the woman whose name on the admission board read Wendy.

Confronting Evil

After blurting out his request, Darren recounted his chaplain visit with Wendy on the locked unit. She engaged him, giving him some insight into her history of sexual abuse at the hands of her parents and her occult involvement (also vis-à-vis her parents). She then explained how she felt harassed by voices that dominated her ability to think and make decisions. Those voices were also telling her to kill herself, which was why she found herself on the locked unit.

At that point, Darren's red flags began to go up. She was seemingly intelligent, in her late twenties, suicidal, with a history of horrible traumas beyond her control. Yet her difficulties didn't fit the normal pattern of delusional or psychotic behavior. The weirdest thing was that Wendy was able to speak objectively and rationally about her problem. Yet *at the same time* she felt helpless to do anything about it.

Finally, Darren shared that Wendy had made a brave request. She asked him to help her with the voices that had been dominating her thoughts for the last ten years. *That* was when things started to get interesting. Someone did not want Darren's assistance, and that someone let him know it.

Without warning, Wendy's face had contorted to an angry scowl, and a growling voice declared, "You cannot take her from us." This was followed by an artful spewing of profanity aimed at Darren, throwing down a challenge to Darren's clear awareness of and insecurity about his identity as God's man—an agent of Jesus Christ. Apparently, the ranking demon had become insecure over Wendy's request and both Darren's *availability* and *ability* to actually help her. In response, he had assumed full control of her to mitigate the threat.

When Darren recognized this personality change, he commanded the spirits to be quiet in the name of Jesus and asked to speak to Wendy only. The demon complied, and Wendy was present again with clarity and faculty and—get this—*completely unaware* of what had just transpired. Darren calmly told her he would be able to help her, but that he was going to need to bring someone with him tomorrow (that's right— yours truly). He gave her some instructions on what to expect and how to prepare. That's when he buzzed himself out of the locked unit and made a beeline to my office.

Driving home from work that day, I skipped my customary bag of fries. The craving for hot grease and salt just wasn't there. The prospect of facing evil *mano a mano* redirected my focus—my mind had been kicked into overdrive. When a man is faced with an imminent deployment to war, his adrenaline pumps, his body gets tense, and his acuity rises to uncommon levels. I was busy matrixing all the pertinent concepts, truths, principles, and accompanying verses in preparation; I began thinking through how to voice my authority in Christ when confronting the demon. I wondered if he knew of me and would speak to me the way he did to Darren.

I had no idea what I was in for.

Yet as I drove, thinking about all this, God's Spirit began to take away the chaos and bring a calming confidence. In the hour it took me to get home, I had revisited God's Word, loaded my ammo magazines, and circled the bases of prayer for Wendy, Darren, and myself. I asked for wisdom to speak to the demon (or demons) effectively like Jesus did. Personally, I recommitted myself to Jesus' authority over my life, I con- fessed and repented of known and unknown sin, and I admitted my inability to do anything without His power. As I pulled into the drive- way and came through the door smelling the dinner I would not eat, one last prayer request hit me—"Lord, prepare Chrissy for this bit of news about to come out of my mouth."

Suffice it to say, I didn't get much sleep that night.

Psychological Warfare

As one might expect, the moment I set foot in the hospital, the mind games started in full swing. It was "game on" for the Enemy and his agents, and they were leaving some big craters, making me pause to look at them:

What's Wendy's attending psychiatrist going to think?

Where are you going to perform this little exorcism?

You are going to put your whole program in jeopardy!

You are going to be laughed at by the clinical staff!

You could lose this contract for your services in the hospital!

How are you going to document *this* in the hospital chart?

What if you are totally wrong about this and the patient is truly delusional or psychotic?

Only a fool would take a risk this great! And for what?

As these invading thought grenades were lobbed into my brain and exploded, you could say I began to suffer a little spiritual shell shock. The steady stream of pounding artillery was unceasing and highly effective. Mind games are mental tactics employed to persuade people to act contrary to the way they originally intended. Sounds evil just by definition, doesn't it? But it's simply good old-fashioned psychological warfare—and the Adversary is well versed in its uses. To this twisted end, Satan and his agents were taking it up a notch.

I was rocked by the realities each of these scenarios presented, and yet I knew there was no turning back. I felt like Lucy Pevensie stepping through the wardrobe closet into another reality. The difference was that in my Narnia, there were no friendly half humans on the other side.

I met Darren in the office, and we immediately began our counterattack—Spirit-guided prayers toward the most critical strongholds within Wendy's mind. We dressed for battle too, strapping on our armor à la Ephesians 6 (we'll dive into this later in the chapters on weapons). Yet most important, we got our buddy armor on. Darren had wisely sought help in the fight: "If one can overpower him who is alone, two can resist him" (Ecclesiastes 4:12, NASB). We exited our office and began walking down the corridor, dressed in armor others could not see, to meet a foe no one else recognized, and to liberate a captive no one else could reach.

Destination: room 302.

First Blood

We greeted Wendy in her room and escorted her to a classroom on the locked unit away from the staff offices and common areas. As we entered, I noticed that there was a blind spot created by the position of the door where we could situate ourselves *and* at the same time insulate ourselves from unwanted looky-loos. Save for some chairs, it was just us three. Sitting down, we began a conversation with Wendy and the agents of evil that would last for over an hour.

"Wendy, do you remember the questions I told you to think over last night?"

"Yes," she said in the softest of voices.

"Is it your desire to be free from these voices and thoughts that you cannot control?"

Again, "Yes."

Darren kept the questions and dialogue directed and steady. "Wendy, do you renounce any and all connections with the occult, Satan, and all his works?" Head bowed, about two feet away, I was coming against the demons, thrones, and powers in the name of Jesus and by His authority commanding them to keep quiet as Darren interacted with Wendy.

Again, "Yes, I do."

Pressing into the real issue, he then focused her and inquired, "Wendy, this is really important. Do you believe that Jesus Christ is the Son of God, that He loves you, died for you, and wants to forgive you and deliver you from evil?"

Again came the "Yes, I do," but this time it was labored and being resisted. Phew! I disciplined myself to stay focused and tie down those forces that would keep Wendy from making a willful and unmolested commitment to Jesus Christ.

"She is ours, and you cannot have her!" he growled through Wendy's gritted teeth.

Darren then began to pray with Wendy, leading her to renounce all attachments with evil in her past and giving herself, her future, and all control in her life over to Jesus Christ. No sooner did she get out the last words of her prayer when the ranking demon manifested himself, reiterating his intentions.

"She is ours, and you cannot have her!" he growled through Wendy's gritted teeth. His hatred of us was plain, and the spirit was more than a little upset over being displaced. His comfortable control now in jeopardy, his days as a squatter in her life were about to end. He had no spiritual right to be there any longer.

Darren and I quickly switched roles. I took over talking, and he started praying. It was an unrehearsed and seamless transition.

"*You* [referring to me] are here to take her away from us," he snarled.

Us! I thought. He meant there was a company of demons in there plaguing this beautiful girl. But at least I had the head honcho.

"What is your name?" I asked. No response, just heavy growling, face to the floor, followed by looks with growling to try to intimidate me.

I repeated, "In the name of Jesus Christ, I command you to tell me your name."

I could see a break in his hold over Wendy's lips when the disgruntled demon replied, "I am Oversayer." Not ironically, his name matched Wendy's chief complaint—dominating voices overriding her own wishes and thoughts, causing confusion, torment, self-abuse, misdiagnoses, and unsuccessful treatment.

"Wendy belongs to Jesus Christ now, and you cannot stay. In the name of Jesus Christ, the One who created you commands you to leave this woman." This was one of the statements that came back to my mind again and again, I think because it reminded all parties of the authority structure and also because, with my limited experience, I needed a simple way of dealing confidently and directly with the demon. I didn't stray far from that focus the entire time.

"You cannot stay. You no longer have authority. Jesus Christ has authority now over Wendy." Whatever else I may have said in that room is lost to me. When I would stop speaking, Darren would jump in. We repeated this in roughly ten-minute shifts with various versions of the same commands for a solid hour. I sensed we needed to keep the pressure on Oversayer to keep him on his heels, and that's exactly what we did until he realized he was going to have to release control of her mind.

Our first sign that something was working came when Wendy suddenly became uncontrolled and violent.

From her seat on the floor, she began to shake hard, as though she were having a seizure. In actuality, I imagine it was the wrenching grip of the ranking demon being extracted by God Himself. He did not want to let go. Oversayer's hooks had been lodged so deeply in Wendy's mind, it took a fair amount of work to pry his long talons out of the recesses and corners of her thoughts. The top half of her body bent from the waist down all the way to the floor, head down and shaking. Then with a loud moan her posture changed. Her body raised itself back with her head now looking straight up at the ceiling.

"I rebuke you in the name of Jesus. Come out of Wendy in the name of Jesus. Leave Wendy in the name of Jesus; she is no longer yours." I continued until there was a loud moan and she fell limp to the floor. Oversayer had finally gotten the boot by Christ. Not really knowing what to do next, Darren jumped in and did what his training in the field had required: check for more demons. All ranking demons have their flocks, and this was no exception as we probed for and called forth any remaining demons. There were many, and these left without dialogue, without incident, and with whimpers like disheartened combatants after their leader gets knocked off. Their evil shepherd was gone.

For the final three rounds, we seemed to develop a pattern. A few more shakes and moans and some more probing for demons. With the final exit, there was no response, just a bewildered young woman staring back at us.

It was over.

Freedom

The look on Wendy's face was of someone searching for something, a thought or an idea. Her eyes were wide open, and her head was slowly turning side to side. Her body language told us she was listening for something. She leaned in toward us, her head tilted. Only it wasn't us she was listening for. We sat silently watching her, and after a minute or so, she finally spoke.

"I can't hear anything." Her voice was weak, stilted. But she sounded cautiously optimistic. "For the first time in ten years I can't hear anything. I don't hear any voices." Part of me wanted to jump up and down, high-five my wing man, and shout in celebration. The other part of me wanted to lie down on the floor.

Then I heard a clear voice say, "Help the poor girl understand what happened and encourage her."

So Darren and I spent the next hour or so explaining step by step what had just transpired. More important, we were able to solidify Wendy's decision to surrender her life to Jesus. This included reading Scripture that spoke specifically about her new position, identity, and connection to Christ. Wendy was like a newborn girl taking baby steps into the freedom that was sealed by the Holy Spirit. We had journeyed back through the wardrobe to leave Narnia, back to the trappings of a locked unit on a mental hospital ward.

And no one was any the wiser. But no one who was in that room that day has been the same since.

Yet as we'll see in the pages that follow, we don't need an up-close, in-your-face demon encounter to join the fight. What we need are God's men who are not apathetic, ambivalent, or indifferent to evil. We can no longer afford to stand idly by and give Satan permission to abuse our brothers and sisters. We must face the reality of evil to stop the two things that most embolden and accelerate Satan's campaigns: the incompetence and passivity of Christ's followers.

We must endeavor to build momentum in the opposite direction, to become intelligent and aggressive evil-fighters.

> *Because one thing the Devil loves is a well-meaning but badly informed Christian.*

Notice "intelligent" *before* "aggressive"? That's crucial. Because one thing the Devil loves is a well-meaning but badly informed Christian.

passion is not enough

There is an old European proverb worth heeding. It reads:
"Age and treachery will always defeat youth and zeal."

—FRANCIS FRANGIPANE

Before we move on to tactical warfare, we need to be well versed in some critical intel. How we approach the Enemy makes all the difference in how we fight and ultimately defeat him.

Consider a parable.

In the fall of 1952 British Royal Navy pilots were baptized, literally, by fire into a new day of aerial combat when they came face to face with the Soviet-made MiG-15 fighter being employed by the North Koreans. The Korean War was in its third year, and news of the encounter (which ended badly for one of the Royal Navy pilots) had traveled fast.

Immediately, flight briefings were called for all carrier-based fighters and pilots. New strategies for fighting the quicker and superior-climbing

MiGs were developed for U.S. pilots, who had a new challenge on their hands. One of the pilots who was listening intently at his briefing was US. Corsair pilot marine Capt. Jesse Folmar. The cold reality facing Folmar and every Corsair pilot was this: the MiG could overwhelm the piston-engined Corsair without difficulty.

Three short weeks after his briefing, Folmar was flying his Corsair toward a target area and preparing for his attack against Korean troops when he and his fellow strike pilot ran into a hornet's nest of seven MiGs. The action went as follows:

Folmar began a turn in his weave when he saw two MiGs in loose eche-lon, heading for the Corsairs. In the next few seconds several things happened. Folmar called, "Tally ho, bandits!" He went to combat power, jettisoned his ordnance and belly tank, and hollered over the guard channel that he was engaged. At the same time he turned toward the threat, telling Daniels (the pilot of the other Corsair) to stay close.

A MiG was diving in astern of Folmar. Daniels broke into it and traded gunfire in a brief head-on pass. The MiG turned left and disengaged, allowing Daniels to reverse his turn and complete his weave off Folmar's starboard beam. While Daniels swapped gunfire with his MiG, Folmar saw two more. They closed rapidly from eight o'clock, and Folmar desperately turned left, trying to bring his guns to bear before the bandits opened fire. But the deflection angle was too great and the closing speed too fast. Tracers passed ahead of Folmar's Corsair, the Reds had over-deflected.

Apparently one MiG passed between Folmar and Daniels. Folmar rolled into a right-hand bank and found the jet in a climbing left turn. The MiG was temporarily vulnerable. "I pulled up, got him in my gunsight, gave him about twenty mils lead, and held a five-second burst," Folmar reported. "I could tell I had him boresighted by the blinking flashes along the left side of the fuselage." The MiG emitted a gray stream of smoke that turned black in seconds. As it pitched down slightly and decelerated, the pilot ejected in a tumbling ball of smoke. Folmar and Daniels could see his G-suit was afire. The flaming jet went vertically into the water from seven thousand feet.[1]

Losing one of their prized MiGs made the North Koreans much more cautious and less aggressive in the months to come in the skies over Korea. The Corsair F4U piston-engined fighter was a dinosaur by the time of the Korean War, but Jesse Folmar's improbable defeat of the faster and nimbler MiG is still spoken of as legend.

Folmar's flaming victim was the last enemy jet to fall to a piston-engined aircraft in the Korean conflict. Air combat analysts credit Folmar's improbable victory to experience, sharp eyes, intelligence, skill, and teamwork with Daniels, combined with the inexperience and lack of familiarity with the MiG on the part of the North Korean pilots.

Go figure. Better, stronger, faster defeated by older, slower, and smarter.

Go figure. Better, stronger, faster defeated by older, slower, and *smarter.*

Jets and Pistons

The MiG-15 *should have* prevailed. That was a given. But while the odds were squarely in the MiG's favor, it was a mistake to underestimate Capt. Jesse Folmar in his Corsair—a big, fat, honking flame ball of a mistake, to be exact. He was outnumbered and outgunned but not *outthought.* I don't know what the Soviet flight instructors were telling their North Korean pupils, but one thing I do know: men will be men. The North Korean pilots were in awe of the MiG's advantages in speed and maneuverability, they were given the intelligence on the top speeds of the Corsair F4U, and they were most likely feeling really good about their odds when they had to strap in for their first missions. New and shiny stuff does things to men. We attach to and believe that we are a reflection of what we possess or drive or fly. Whether it's a Mercedes or a MiG, we *are* our accessories.

Right?

This is a particularly male flaw, and it's commonly fatal. No doubt, it was part of the dynamic with the North Korean pilots. They thought they would be invincible. How could they not be? The MiG was built up in their minds to be invincible against the Stone-Age aircraft the Americans were flying. In any group of men, these kinds of testosterone-induced thoughts can build upon each other at light speed:

- They won't even see us coming.
- The Americans will be slow-moving targets.
- I'm going to get the first one.
- We have jets, and they have pistons.
- We're going to win the war for our country and be heroes!

So now shift back to engaging with evil. In this parable, we are the MiGs. God's man is better equipped for the fight, and he *should* prevail. We love our position in Christ. We love His victory over Satan at the Cross. We are enthusiastic. We have the best armor and weapons.

But like the North Koreans, we are outtested and outthought by the Devil. He should not prevail, but he is winning most of his dogfights with men in the body of Christ. He should not have air superiority, but tactically he is better at his game, and he'll fight to the death. He's causing God's men to bail out on their marriages, compromise their faith, abandon their discipline, and question their commitment to Christ. Sadly, the skies above this war are raining parachutes and tumbling balls of smoke.

> *We attach to and believe that we are a reflection of what we possess or drive or fly. Whether it's a Mercedes or a MiG, we are our accessories. Right? This is a particularly male flaw, and it's commonly fatal.*

Remember, these are men who climbed into their cockpits full of energy and zeal. Their faith in victory took off like a supersonic jet only to get shot out of the sky by an old piston-engined fighter.

The Devil is one crafty veteran.

Satan is legendary for his ability to take down the best of men who began their journey with Christ fully equipped with all the resources of God and the best of intentions. Get that. *We have to see just how good he is at this in order to raise our respect and awareness to where it needs to be.* While ownership of the spiritual resources for our dogfight with evil is guaranteed, that does not mean possession of or mastery over or victory in our fight on earth. Zeal and equipment are not enough.

It seems almost every week I hear of another leader or fellow pastor in God's army who has been shot down after what seemed to be an awesome beginning. Their stories follow an eerily familiar pattern:

* highly visible conversion
* accelerated spiritual growth and training

- visionary aspiration
- strong spiritual gifting and willingness to risk
- clear call to service to and ministry for Christ
- growing responsibilities of leadership in the body of Christ
- success and recognition
- growing pressures connected to their responsibilities
- growing frustrations and discouragements
- increasing isolation from others and openness to small spiritual compromises
- spiritual footholds established by the Enemy; growth of private sin
- compromise in relationships with God and people
- undisclosed private struggles in the midst of public success
- sin-induced cynicism and callousness
- isolation from others and fierce resistance to accountability
- increased vulnerability to outside assault
- discontent and loss of vision for ministry and service
- acceptance of habitual sin to medicate spiritual despair
- and eventually, a giant fireball trailing thick black smoke and headed toward earth

For these men and others like them, their sin did not bring about their fall; it was their *lack of discernment and understanding of their foe.* Somewhere along the way God's man

- compartmentalized the evil
- made the Enemy an abstract theological construct
- ignored God's warnings
- and never saw the Devil coming.

Early in their spiritual quest, they saw Satan as a huge threat. But now, with victory over major sins, some spiritual growth and success, and a little knowledge about God to flex in front of others, the threat level was lowered to condition Green, low risk.

> *Their sin did not bring about their fall; it was their lack of discernment and understanding of their foe.*

Perfect.

Yet simultaneously, Satan rolled into a right-hand bank and found our God's man temporarily vulnerable.

Satan fired the shots, but *ignorance* was the real culprit.

Flight Briefing

Drafted unexpectedly by Jesus, Peter and Andrew left it all to travel and train with a Man who told them they would be one day fishing for men. That conversation by the Sea of Galilee seemed like a distant memory now because of the rapid escalation and popularity of Jesus' ministry. They had witnessed Jesus' first Sermon on the Mount, seen Him reach out to the leper, applaud the faith of a centurion, command a storm, raise a dead girl, and make a cripple walk, and who could forget the demon-possessed man of Gadara—one word from Jesus' lips and a herd of pigs plunge themselves into a lake!

Man, oh, man.

This whole time they were learning the art of war, how to advance the kingdom amid hostile men of all persuasions—religious, political, cultural, and satanic. He was showing them how a compassionate God's man fights during his time on earth: teaching, preaching, healing, and boldly liberating those who are held captive and controlled by the god of this world and by sin. But now their residency was coming to an end. The season of selection, association, and demonstration was giving way to the next phase: *delegation and supervision.* He looked at them and said, "The harvest is plentiful but the workers are few. Ask the Lord of the harvest, therefore, to send out workers into his harvest field" (Matthew 9:37).

This "flight briefing" called by the Master Instructor went exactly like this:

He called His twelve disciples to Him and "gave them authority to drive out evil spirits and to heal every disease and sickness." He told them, "As you go, preach this message: 'The kingdom of heaven is near.' Heal the sick, raise the dead, cleanse those who have leprosy, drive out demons. Freely you have received, freely give.... I am sending you out like sheep among wolves. Therefore be as shrewd as snakes and as inno-cent as doves" (Matthew 10:1, 7–8, 16). Now that's what I call a green light! With the full endorsement of the Supreme Commander, God's men were given

- a sanction to fight ("gave them authority")
- a message to forward ("preach this")
- targets to find (sick, dead, lepers, demon possessed)
- power to free (to heal, raise, cleanse, and drive out)
- a charge to feel ("freely you have received, freely give")
- a metaphor to familiarize ("sending you out like sheep among wolves")
- two commands to fulfill ("be shrewd" and "innocent")

Imagine you are there. Which of these would send your neurons into high gear?

When the army air cavalry are dropped into a neck of woods that will be filled with metal from the get-go, it's called a "hot LZ" (landing zone). This means *it's hostile the moment they land.* These are the kinds of announcements that get soldiers puking the closer they get. And if they're not puking, the helicopter blades rotating in their stomachs match the real ones pound for pound emotionally.

Every instruction up to then had to feel good to the disciples before that announcement. This condition of hostility would not change for these men until they were martyred. Jesus didn't provide false hope or codependent comfort. He gave it to them straight—this was the campaign to rid the world of Satan's grip through kingdom advance. And He didn't say, "You'll be sheep among wolves for a while." He meant it for life.

Think about wolves for a second:

- They eat sheep.
- They hunt in packs.
- They're beautiful animals with sharp, pointy teeth.
- They have a wicked sense of smell.
- They're smart, stealthy, and deadly.

And you don't want to be caught alone against the pack.

Take this in, God's man: You are a sheep among wolves *right now.* And you will remain among them going forward here on earth until you get called back to the office of the Supreme Commander for debriefing.

One of the main reasons we are getting massacred is that we are sheep among wolves, but we act like sheep among squirrels. We go along in this world as if there were no hostility—and no war zone! "What bombs? What enemy? What destruction? What blood? Bondage? Affairs? Divorce? Fatherlessness? Shattered lives? Oh, that. Yeah, it's a pity. Hey, did you want diet or regular Coke with that plate of denial?"

> *One of the main reasons we are getting massacred is that we are sheep among wolves, but we act like sheep among squirrels.*

That kind of ignorance is the definition of spiritual dysfunction.

Still, sane men who call attention to these evil-sponsored campaigns are considered goofy, and the goofy men playing with the squirrels are considered sane. This dysfunctional view of the spiritual battle makes those who are fighting justifiably frustrated by those who aren't. "Today," says Bono (of U2), "it's a load of sissies running around with their 'bless me' clubs. And there's a war going on between good and evil. Millions of children and millions of lives are being lost to greed, to bureaucracy, and to a church that's been asleep. And it sends me out of my mind with anger."[2]

You can just feel the frustration and, at the same time, Satan's elation. "That's right," he sighs. "Just harmless little squirrels."

You want more? Even now I can see Satan bending over your shoulder: "What is this Luck guy all jacked up about? Bono? Seriously, he's your theologian? Relax. Chill. Put the book down, and grab that Diet Coke."

He's not just really smooth, he wants you to let him remain hidden and believe he's no threat. Don't let him lie to you. Listen to Jesus: it's *wolves, not squirrels.*

Snake-Doves

An odd combination, but when you put them together with *shrewd* and *innocent,* snakes and doves start to make sense. Jesus knew if His men were going to be fighting it out in a hot LZ, they were going to need great intel and a pure heart *to translate* that intel into action. According to Jesus, wisdom and carefulness (shrewdness) combined with virtue and integrity (innocence) would give them the ability to know what to do next and the right stuff to pull it off. These two traits had to be there before heading off to war against evil.

A shrewd God's man will

- take the ax to personal sin
- fiercely guard and preserve his spiritual gains
- exercise discernment in all situations impacting his relationships with God and people
- not allow negative emotions to fester and play into the Enemy's plans
- possess good intelligence on his enemy
- pick his battles carefully so as not to waste energy
- cleverly de-escalate internal conflicts to bring peace
- root out diversions, distractions, and doubts that cloud issues
- act quickly and decisively when needed

When you think "shrewd," you think *perceptive* and *not naive.* Perfect preparation before going into war. In other words, "Be clear about your mission, be intentional, and don't compromise it by getting lazy—or else." The same command is now put to you, God's man, as we prepare to go forward into the fight. Right now, Jesus is telling you, *"Stay sharp, on purpose, and don't get sucker-punched! Be shrewd as a snake, and sense the battle on the scales of your spirit, feel the vibrations, and play it smart, because to outwit a serpent you gotta think like one. He's crafty and smart. Don't be outthought!"*

Be shrewd.

Then, to your spiritual shrewdness add innocence. An innocent God's man will

- seek to keep his heart clean before God so he can hear His voice
- openly examine himself before God *and* man—no secrets
- hate evil and run from it if necessary to preserve his integrity
- control himself to keep polluting influences out of his relationship with God
- become increasingly unsullied by his old ways of living
- put strong boundaries in his life to preempt evil assaults
- control his thoughts and not allow any that are outside the will of God
- soak his mind in God's thoughts and desires
- seek aggressive accountability and use it to win his battles with evil

Jesus knew that innocence to evil and sin was the secret to clarity of mind and receptivity to His Spirit in battle. Compromises of the mind and heart create interrupting static that hinders the effective communication necessary when fighting "bandits" of the air. Imagine a radioman on the front who is unable to call in mortar rounds because his cable has been cut or his signal is being jammed. Personal purity of mind, body, and devotion add up to our assurance of battlefield acuity and ability. Innocence to evil, according to Jesus, means more impact in the fight against it.

Be innocent.

Jesus is intentional with His men as He prepares them for war. He calls them to wisdom before warfare and virtue before victory. As for us, our personal commitment to train in wisdom and commit to spiritual integrity is critical. Our King always demanded the real deal: "Why do you call me, 'Lord, Lord,' and do not do what I say?" (Luke 6:46). To fight with Jesus means to be all in, hands stacked on His, eyes locked, and agreed that we will take this fight to the last breath—no shortcuts. Versus what? Half in with the keys to the back door in your pocket in case things get uncomfortable. He also desired His fighters to *actively defer to and be directed by* divine wisdom and realities over their own. He prayed over us, "Sanctify them by the truth; your word is truth" (John 17:17). A spiritually shrewd man is a man of the Word.

Last, He said there would be a direct link between our personal purity of heart and our ability to experience God's presence: "Blessed are the pure in heart, for they will see God" (Matthew 5:8). On the battlefield, your team needs good communication, good hand signals, and a connected intuition. This kind of nonverbal and spontaneous communication is life and breath to a fighting unit amid suppression fire, heavy artillery, and bloody hand-to-hand combat. Innocence to evil along with spiritual integrity takes the worry of internal conflict out of play. They put you above the noise to enable you to tune out Satan's temptations and manipulative distractions.

So remember, passion for the fight is clearly not enough. According to our Master Instructor, *shrewdness and innocence are the key intuitive qualities required to fight evil consistently and effectively.* They cannot be in short supply in a fighting God's man. Satan's age and treachery defeat spiritual youth and zeal every time. The evidence is all around us. God's men don't finish strong, because they underestimate Satan, put him in a mental box, and are beaten when he doesn't stay there. But when wisdom and purity combine with zeal for Christ, victory is definitely within reach.

In taking the fight to the Enemy, it's the snake-doves who have the upper hand on Mr. Wolf.

that one thing

To knock a thing down, especially if it is cocked at an arrogant angle, is a deep delight of the blood.

—GEORGE SANTAYANA

"What a waste."

That's what we say when we have known someone who was bright, talented, competent, and highly skilled, *but* (say it slowly) *one thing* about the person's character got in the way. The one obstacle. After achieving great success, *that one thing* is the very thing that can sabotage everything he or she worked so hard to achieve.

Think Michael Vick.

On the national stage, football fans fell in love with Michael Vick's abilities in the BCS National Championship game against Florida State in January 2000. Even though his team lost, the world had never seen such potential at the quarterback position. The kid throws for 225 yards and *runs* for 95 more while scoring two touchdowns himself. In 2001, he leads his team to a 41–20 victory over Clemson and is named MVP of the game. As predicted, in April of that year he is selected in the first round of the NFL draft by the Atlanta Falcons and with the stroke of a pen becomes a multimillionaire. Michael Vick's career over the next five years is nothing short of liquid "nitro" plus a match. He is, as ESPN's Dan Patrick likes to exclaim, *"en fuego"*:

- three Pro Bowl selections
- three play-off appearances
- an NFC South title
- an NFC title-game appearance
- a new contract worth $130 million

Then there's that one thing.

The year 2006 was a disappointing season for Mike Vick and the Falcons, who failed to live up to their preseason hype. They do not make the play-offs, compiling a mediocre record with only seven wins to nine losses, and the shining star of the Falcons is booed off the field after a season-ending loss to the Saints. Walking to the exit, he lets the fans know exactly how he feels by making the universal gesture that says, "Boo *this*!" Frosting on the cake. That one thing costs him thousands of dollars in the form of a fine by the NFL and earns him the privilege of making a public apology. Although people are disappointed, the public cannot see the growing cancer inside a man who has need of nothing but is on the verge of losing everything because of, you guessed it, *that one thing*. Just five months later, the fuel tanks fall off Michael Vick's space shuttle, and gravity wins.

Terminal velocity is reached in the spring and summer of 2007. The Associated Press chronicled for the nation chapter one of the deconstruction of Michael Vick:

- April 27: Police and animal-control officers find a dog-training complex behind Vick's house along with sixty-six dogs on the property.
- July 2: An illegal dog-fighting operation has been operating on Vick's property for the past five years.
- July 17: The U.S. attorney's office announces that Vick and three friends have been indicted.
- July 19: Shoe giant Nike suspends all Vick products and eventually terminates his endorsement deal.
- July 26: Vick and his codefendants plead not guilty.
- July 30: A codefendant reaches a plea deal with prosecutors in exchange for his testimony against Vick.
- August 17: Two other codefendants reach plea deals with prosecutors.
- August 20: Michael Vick's attorney says he will enter a guilty plea.
- August 28: Michael Vick pleads guilty before a federal judge and shortly after apologizes "for all the things that I've done and that I've allowed to happen." He adds, "Through this situation I have found Jesus," and vowed to redeem himself. "I have to."[1]

Professionally, this is a titanic disaster for Vick. Personally, it looks like the beginning of a painful but corrective surgery of character and, hopefully, the successful removal of that one thing that sabotaged his success. As Vick himself put it as he left the press conference, "I got a lot of down time to think about my actions." Like an instant Polaroid snapshot that starts out blurry and formless, a picture began to take shape, highlighting a core facet of Michael Vick that the public was not allowed to see. For the first time, the public saw a picture of his character, the *real man* beneath the freakish athletic skills. And when the hidden details coalesced, the lies were retracted and the lines were retraced. And the real picture revealed that Vick's affluence and influence *outpaced* his character's ability to manage it. It wasn't so much that he did a bad thing (we are all one step away from stupid). It was his ignorance of that one part of himself that became his worst enemy—the part that tolerated darkness. One thing—pride—gave access to the darkness.

Whatever your opinion of Michael Vick, don't do one thing: don't gloat.

No Dark Corners

We each have a key task to complete before we set out to fight evil: discerning the darkness in our own hearts. Jesus said, "Make sure that the light you think you have is not really darkness. If you are filled with light, with no dark corners, then your whole life will be radiant, as though a floodlight is filling you with light" (Luke 11:35–36, NLT 1996). This shot across the bow is directed by Jesus Himself at *Christians*! He knew this one thing would be critical for His followers: the strange dynamic of how faith gets hijacked by evil. It's a terrifying thought, Jesus' telling us we'll have to actively evaluate ourselves to keep from becoming an unwitting pawn for evil. But if it's true that Christians can be doing God's work, shining His light, *and simultaneously* be providing a safe haven for darkness, we have some heart investigation to do.

To understand the full implications of Jesus' words here, first we have to realize that He knows all about Satan's domain of existence. Jesus was present when Satan and the angels rebelled and were consigned to darkness: "I remind you of the angels who did not stay within the limits of authority God gave them but left the place where they belonged. God has kept them securely chained in prisons of darkness, waiting for the great day of judgment" (Jude 6, NLT 2004). Satan has been forced to live in darkness away from the presence of God's light. Second, this darkness is not physical but moral. Third, Satan has the freedom to traffic his schemes and sow destruction *anywhere* moral darkness is tolerated. He can search out, invade, and thrive in both the small spaces harboring darkness in a person's mind as well as in large and obvious spaces. The common denominator is the moral darkness there. An attitude, an action, a way of thinking, or a way of living are all possible places of moral darkness *and,* by definition of his sentence, a place where Satan is free to traffic, transport, and transact evil. Unfortunately, most believers compartmentalize this truth and believe this darkness is a place *beyond* them in some other realm.

No. He is bound to be wherever darkness abides.

Jesus' warning to His men not only demonstrates His insight into how evil and darkness can invade the goodness and light of any believer, it should have also caused the disciples to pause and reflect on the personal implications. It's an admonition to God's man to step back, take a look at himself objectively, and ask the hard questions about the motives behind *why* he is doing what he's doing for Christ. Specifically: is it about *me* or about *Him?*

It's a caution flag for those mustangs among us (me, for example) who would subconsciously put their own plans ahead of God's and pawn them off as God's plan, à la Peter. Jesus was putting all disciples on red alert against the dark corners of sin, pride, fear, and other unexamined or ignored character dysfunctions that could make them vulnerable to attack in the midst of their ministry. Any number of Christian leaders could testify to this very dynamic of self-destruction. We all are prone to getting stuck, bound to something *inside us* that could easily undermine our best intentions.

How many fallen Christian leaders were seemingly untouchable up on those pedestals and no one ever put two and two together? People forgot they were mere men, and God allowed these pseudomessiahs to be broken of their pride and presumption. They allowed the darkness to coexist with their faith while also representing Christ—a darkness they either didn't understand or were unconvinced would destroy them—so God allowed the Enemy to have his way with them just as He did with His own disciples. For many of these leaders this meant public outings and loss of influence and income, of leadership positions, of reputations, of marriages and entire ministries.

Seemingly radiant, shining floodlights were snuffed out and forced to realize that God does not buy prideful rationalization of sin. The *one thing* inside them accommodating darkness let Satan loose in their lives. This common belief, this twisted perception of reality, is a danger for any God's man, persuading him consciously or subconsciously to become a law to himself and permit a dark attitude or action to remain in his life.

> **fight fact**
> *When you harbor sin, you become a courier for darkness, and God will not entrust the kingdom fight or work to such a man. Instead, you will get worked.*

It is, quite literally, a deal with the Devil.

He will allow you to be *sifted* by Satan himself or by a trial or circumstance. Whatever it takes to break the foothold of pride and self-sufficiency out of you. Got your attention? Remember, Satan is allowed to be wherever darkness is welcomed. And pride is like a sky-banner invitation to come to your party.

Get this. *Really* get this. Let it sink in. Change the way you look at yourself and how Satan works against you personally. Because until you do, you will be missing the most important piece of intel you can have—*the one about you!*

Pastor Francis Frangipane understands the confusion most Christians face over Satan's presence, but he doesn't protect us from the cold, hard fact about Satan's freedom to set up shop in any dark space: "Many Christians debate whether the devil is on earth or in hell; can he dwell in Christians or only in the world? The fact is, the devil is in the darkness. Wherever there is spiritual darkness, there the devil will be."

And now you know.

The Darkness Within

God's man can unwittingly, unknowingly, or ignorantly partner with the Devil.

For this reason, we can't go freewheeling into the topics of and training for spiritual battle without first dealing with the guy in the mirror. It doesn't matter how closely you have walked with God in the past, how fervently you are walking with Jesus in the present, how many mission trips you have been on, or how many messages you have preached. Every week at Every Man Ministries (EMM) we hear about or are asked to help another God's man who has bit the dust because Satan is trafficking some of his best stuff in and through some of *our best men*! Yeah. Go figure. So look in the mirror and don't say, "Nope, not me." Take a closer look and consider that even Peter the Rock was blind to the darkness in him. Compare your spiritual résumé with his:

- He walked alongside the Son of God for three years.
- He performed miraculous healings.
- He cast out demons.
- He was first in the water when Jesus came walking to the disciples in the boat.
- He was the first disciple to recognize Jesus as Messiah.
- He threw the first punch (a sword swipe really) at the Roman soldiers when they came for Jesus (my personal favorite).
- He was told by Jesus that the church would be built on *his* shoulders.
- He was told by Jesus that he'd wear a crown in heaven and reign with Him for all eternity.

And yet Jesus *intentionally* permitted Peter to be to be sifted and cleansed of a darkness (pride) he was oblivious to before He allowed him to take his place among God's men managing the kingdom responsibilities in the book of Acts.

> *All God's men who will fight evil must pause and reflect on how our Commander feels about character preceding influence.*

Why? Because lurking just beneath the surface of Peter's award-winning commitment to Christ was *that one thing.* This God's man, like a lot of us, had the competitive and risk-taking personality wired into his hard drive. But with Jesus, outward expression was always second to inner purity. *That one thing,* that aspect of Peter that would get in the way of all that passion, commitment, and energy, was leaking and visible. In Luke 22, we see it come out, and Jesus addresses it in a weird and ominous way. All God's men who will fight evil must pause and reflect on how our Commander feels about character preceding influence.

They began to argue among themselves as to who would be the greatest in the coming kingdom. Jesus told them,

> "In this world the kings and great men order their people around, and yet they are called 'friends of the people.' But among you, those who are the greatest should take the lowest rank, and the leader should be like a servant. Normally the master sits at the table and is served by his servants. But not here! For I am your servant. You have remained true to me in my time of trial. And just as my Father has granted me a Kingdom, I now grant you the right to eat and drink at my table in that Kingdom. And you will sit on thrones, judging the twelve tribes of Israel.
>
> "Simon, Simon, Satan has asked to have all of you, to sift you like wheat. But I have pleaded in prayer for you, Simon, that your faith should not fail. So when you have repented and turned to me again, strengthen and build up your brothers."
>
> Peter said, "Lord I am ready to go to prison with you, and even to die with you." (Luke 22:25–33, NLT 1996)

Praying for me against Satan? When I repent and turn back to Him? Peter's stomach must have clenched up real tight, his mind must have started racing, his defenses and insecurities skyrocketing to Code Red. This is the definition of an awkward moment. "Uh, sorry, Jesus. I was just staking my claim." At this point, Peter was the most high-profile disciple on the team. He'd just been guaranteed a starring role in eternity. And just as they're sharing this intimate moment, *THWACK!* Jesus pours water on the "Rock-star." We now know who's going to be the greatest by whom Satan is asking to sift. But Peter's sense of self is demolished momentarily, and his joy is interrupted. "Satan asked for permission to sift *me,* and You said *yes?* Why me? What about our history? And what about all the talk about the Good Shepherd protecting His sheep? What's going on?"

A few long seconds pass. Peter's brain is crunching the data. Then his response, "Fine. Bring it on. I'll prove I'm all that." Predictably proud, ambitious, and self-sufficient, Peter can't help himself. Whether it's the awkwardness of the moment, his false sense of self, or ignorance about just how severe his sifting process would be, *that one thing* leaks out. It's like he's wearing a Day-Glo T-shirt that reads SIFT ME in big block letters and he doesn't know it.

Jesus says, "Satan has asked to sift *all of you.*" He needed more than an impulsive risk taker who would eat a cockroach whole on His request. Satan wanted a shot at Peter's inner man and the opportunity to challenge his true self under pressures he had not yet faced *alone* as God's man. While Satan wanted a shot at Peter, Jesus was engineering a surgery.

Sifting Before Service

Mention sifting to a first-century Jew, and he immediately gets an image, much like we think of downloading in our age of digital technology. Jesus spins the term *sifting* here into the spiritual process Peter is about to experience at the hands of Satan.

Peter Googles *sifting* in his mind, and up pops the picture on his mental screen:

- big wood-box frame
- screen on the bottom
- a man on either side rapidly shaking the frame

- dirt and chaff falling to the ground
- pure kernels of wheat on top

The bad and the useless fall off, and the good stuff remains. *But why me?* he thought. The problem was that he had no idea what was coming. He had no clue how violent God would allow his sifting to be to get *that one thing* to fall to the ground. He'd be used by God in all the ways Jesus promised, but only *after* the sifting, *after* the purification of his character. Jesus knew Peter would be an easy mark for Satan if certain impurities in him were not removed first, so He had to break him before He could bless him in his service for God. The pride had to go.

Here's how it happened for Peter:

- Christ's boldest defender denies Him three times, bowing to pressure from a little girl and cursing as he denies his connection to Jesus.
- Peter is convinced by Satan that he's unworthy of Jesus' promises to him.
- Though he sees the resurrected Christ, he self-selects *out* of leadership and goes back to fishing.
- Jesus comes to find him, proves Himself to Peter once more, and Peter jumps out of the boat to swim for shore.
- Jesus fixes him breakfast and asks him a few questions designed to help Peter remember that his connection to Jesus is unbreakable. Peter's insecurity falls to the ground, and only his true loyalty to and love for Christ are left.

And finally, Jesus stops shaking the sieve. Peter must have felt something of how Edmund felt in C.S. Lewis's *The Lion, the Witch and the Wardrobe* after betraying his brothers and sisters: like a loser given a second chance and made into a prince.

Sifting is synonymous with elimination. What Peter could not recognize in *himself*, God eliminated. He allowed Peter to be selected and exposed

> *Sifting is synonymous with elimination.*

to a trial and testing that would *separate* and *eliminate* his ego from his service for Christ, deconstruct the old Peter, and raise up a new man with a new *character*. There is no longer a place for darkness to dwell in his life. It has been replaced with the light of the character of Christ Himself—an impenetrable force.

Surgical Strike

So what's going on inside of you? *That* is more critical to victory in the bigger fight than whatever words you're saying. Look at Peter, and then look at yourself. If you want to become an easy mark for Satan, simply deny, excuse, or rationalize this. But if you want to play a key part in the battle, consider the dark footholds of sin, pride, or fear you're having trouble letting go of

- an arrogant or self-centered spirit
- a growing materialistic tendency
- overconcern with titles, status, or position
- an addiction to approval
- a secret sexual sin
- an overreaction to criticism
- emotional reliance upon past successes
- closemindedness or an unteachable spirit
- an unwillingness to be accountable to others
- a disregard for core spiritual disciplines
- a disconnectedness from your spouse
- behaviors that isolate you from other Christians

- harbored resentments or unforgiveness
- a critical spirit
- discontentment, jealousy, or envy
- defensiveness
- disrespect of others
- an attitude of entitlement and lack of humility
- permitting questionable behaviors

All of these are examples of *that one thing* with one common denominator: dangerous darkness of character. They're all connected to your morality, dragging it down when you're being friendly with darkness. But watch out. If you've made a commitment to Christ, Satan will be allowed to come against you in an area of weakness until you realize that God desires the dark corners in your character are to be eliminated. He wants you proactive in your battle against pride—to shut the door on all dark attitudes. It's when God's man *assimilates the character of Christ* in a dark area that the Devil withdraws. Only then will Satan know that *you know* all circumstances, trials, and sifting only work to perfect and complete you as God's man.

In times of sifting, a fighting faith is produced, pure and unassailable. And if you respond decisively, Satan will be forced to abandon his sabotage as Christ's own nature in you successfully walls off those dark aspects of your inner construction.

Of deep delight to God is when a believer cooperates with Him in knocking sin, pride, and presumption down on a regular basis and keeps darkness on the run. It's not something that will go away by itself or once and for all. It requires an inner discipline and diligent management. To deny darkness its ability to traffic through you, you must be willing to *continually* explore the dark spaces of your own heart, look at them clearly, and resolve to deal with them dramatically (see Mark 9:43–50 on taking bold steps in this direction).

The result? God can then entrust you with the weightier responsibilities of His kingdom. In the kingdom's theaters of spiritual battle, the men who get deployed to the battle lines *out there* have already dealt with the terrorist cell *in here* (tap your chest for me).

Go after *that one thing.*

Now is the perfect time to ask God to show you what needs to be eliminated so you can fight successfully with power and wisdom. We are all works in progress, and we all have blind spots. Ask your spouse or a good friend (God's spotters) if they see in you any of the tendencies on that list. And remember that all God has is wounded warriors, so there's no reason for you to be any different. You can be in this fight as long you're clean on the inside (meditate on 2 Timothy 2:20–22 for more along these lines). And if you're being sifted right now, remember that sifting produces your usefulness for this fight!

With no dark corners to work in, the Enemy doesn't stand a chance.

Note: For more in-depth character alignment, check out *Dream* and the *Dream Workbook,* the second step in the God's Man series.

Part 2

discerning evil

night vision

If we had to meet the devil, and knew him to be what he is, we might far more easily conquer him; but we have to deal with him disguised as an angel of light, and here is the need of a hundred eyes, each one of them opened by God, that we may see.

— CHARLES HADDON SPURGEON

You are about to cross a line.

Ever had someone tell you, "I don't want to alarm you, but…"? They always proceed to tell you something that triggers your fight-or-flight response.

Well, I don't want to alarm you, but…we have reached that point.

This section of *Fight* will move you beyond acknowledging evil and toward a deeper and more intimate knowledge of the Evil One—his character, his guises, his helpers, his tactics, and his fears. The events in my life prior to writing this section made it obvious to me that the

Enemy wants more than anything to kill off God's man and keep you from receiving the night-vision goggles described in the following chapters. He has unleashed a Kenny-focused barrage of distraction, interruption, commotion, and mental disruption unlike anything I've ever experienced as a servant of Christ. Why, then, should we not expect him to be equally focused on you while you read this actionable intelligence? I hope you're ready to pick a fight with evil because it's coming your way now. There's no reason he won't attack your mind and life in ways similar to what he's done in mine.

> *The fangs are out. The cavalry has been called. The bullets are flying. Sacrifices must be made.*

His reactions have made me realize even more deeply how important his stake in you is and how intense the reality of the ongoing fight is. The fangs are out. The cavalry has been called. The bullets are flying. Sacrifices must be made. The resolve of both sides has stiffened. The Enemy knows that the insights that follow will reveal him for who he really is, and after we connect the pieces, *the game will change for him.*

My friend Paul, a retired USMC F-18 pilot, says, "The enemy can hear you coming, but he can't see you, so he will throw out a wall of lead called 'barrage fire' hoping you will run into it. The closer you get to the target, the more resistance there is. When you experience the resistance, it should cause increased vigilance." The resistance I have experienced in getting to this place has been dramatically amplified, so I am doing three things. First, I am stiffening my resolve and increasing my vigilance. Second, I am committing to pressing into the fight. Third, I am warning you of what's coming.

Expect a wall of lead.

The Single Greatest Mismatch

Gen. Barry McCaffrey, then commander of the Twenty-fourth Infantry Division, identified how Operation Desert Storm was tipped dramatically in favor of the Americans and their allies when he observed, "Our night vision capability provided the single greatest mismatch of war."

Case in point was Joe McMaster and his Quick Reaction Force (QRF) team who "owned the night." His camp came under mortar fire from "outside the wire," beyond the perimeter of the base camp. When this happened, McMaster's QRF team was mobilized and sent out to locate and destroy the enemy. "We were 400 feet away and they had no clue that we were there. On the other hand we could see the enemy, plain as day." According to Dr. Robert Wiseman, former head of Night Vision Command, when night vision was first being deployed in Vietnam, grateful soldiers would tell the staff, "You don't know how many lives you've saved."

There are parallel spiritual truths here for us in facing resistance and hostile fire:

- The ability to see the enemy and maneuver in the darkness provides a *huge* tactical advantage.
- The ability to respond effectively and productively *when attacked* provides confidence.
- The ability to rescue, defend, and save lives provides incentive to use night vision more.

Night vision is to modern warfare what *discernment* is to your effectiveness against evil. In this section, I want to supply you with the intimate knowledge Satan fears having publicized and integrated into your life. I know he hates what we're going to address because he devotes so much time and energy spreading disinformation about his MO. But when he goes from being a blip on your radar to being a highly recognizable priority threat, it frustrates and angers him to no end. Worse yet, when we focus on applying the intel, there's no telling what he may do in his rage.

Borrowing from the comments by soldiers using night vision in combat, ask yourself:

- How valuable is the ability to see an invisible enemy by taking away his cover of darkness?
- How useful is the ability to respond, locate, and neutralize threats quickly?
- How disconcerting do you think it is to a terrorist organization when all its fake identities, safe houses, fronting businesses, weapons caches, terrorist cells, and its ultimate, secret playbook are intercepted and disseminated?
- How helpful would it be to know the psychology of your enemy leader, his motivations, and the resulting tactics?

For our enemy, remaining incognito is priority one, but we're going to expose his masquerade on as many levels as possible. Oh yes, you can believe he's hot under the collar about this desire of yours, and he's going to see to it that it goes one place: nowhere. That's why, to employ God's night-vision capability and direct it at Satan, you're going to need more than passion and a game plan against pride. You're going to need the up-to-the-minute intel on the ground this section will provide. When you act on this information, your offensive will be rock solid, incapable of being compromised. And this should provide the supreme confidence that your efforts will be rewarded with victories.

In this fight, it's the intel that will prove fatal for our foe.

> For the LORD gives wisdom; from His mouth come knowledge and understanding. He stores up sound wisdom for the upright; He is a shield to those who walk in integrity, guarding the paths of justice, and He preserves the way of His godly ones. Then you will discern righteousness and justice and equity and every good course. For wisdom will enter your heart, and knowledge will be pleasant to your soul; *discretion will guard you, understanding will watch over you, to deliver you from the way of evil.* (Proverbs 2:6–12, NASB)

God's night vision will provide

- protection: "He stores up sound wisdom for the upright [and] is a *shield*"
- preservation: "He preserves the way of His godly ones"
- intuition: "Then you will discern righteousness"
- admonition: "Discretion will guard you, understanding will watch over you"
- liberation: "To deliver you from the way of evil"

God is going to supply you with tried-and-true spiritual technology so that you can see and respond to evil effectively. And He's ready to do it.

Your part?

Integrity Adds Clarity

God doesn't waste His wisdom. He engineered it to only activate inside a man who is committed to Christlike character. That's why my book

Dream preceded *Fight,* to lay the essential foundation of Christlike character for the intel to activate.

Notice that He doesn't give just anyone living wisdom for the fight. He looks for the difference between intellectual understanding and practical application. I know lots of guys, pastors, and full-time theologians who have been exposed to the wisdom God provides, but they are still getting slaughtered by the Enemy. The Bible says that the more spiritually undivided you are, the better your intel gets. The more integrity, the more clarity. Don't miss the phraseology of the way God's intelligence community operates real time: "He stores up sound wisdom for the upright...is a shield to those who walk in integrity.... He preserves the way of His godly ones." The wisdom the Bible provides is there for every believer, but the Scriptures are quick to point out that *having information* and *acting on it* are two different things. The difference comes in integration and depends entirely on the character of the soldier. That's what God looks for.

My buddy Paul, "F-18 man," put this into perspective when he told me about the mechanics of night vision. "Night-vision goggles take ambient light from the stars and moon and amplify it. If there's no light, there's no sight." The spiritual implication? If the light of Christ isn't present in your life, you will not see the Enemy, or the ground, before you crash. Spiritual night vision requires available light *in you* before it can be amplified to help win a fight. The ambient light of your spiritual character comes from rooting out darkness in internal strongholds and allowing God's Word to illuminate your mind. And it's crucial, as you move forward, that spiritual preparation and inventory should be taken to gauge your "amplification ratio." To gain sight for the battle, you must be a man of light.

"If we claim to have fellowship with him yet *walk in the darkness,* we lie and do not live by the truth. But if we walk in the light, as he is in the light, we have fellowship with one another, and the blood of Jesus, his Son, purifies us from all sin. If we claim to be without sin, we deceive ourselves and the truth is not in us" (1 John 1:6–8).

So be aware: the advantage God's night vision provides for the fight is only as strong as the light your character maintains. If publicly you talk a good game but privately you compartmentalize and practice sin, all bets are off. Put the book down and go back to square one. Confess and repent of darkness (attitude or actions), and start to build back the light.

God's message is crystal clear: how can a man discern the darkness when he's shaking hands with it in one form or another? There's something wrong with that picture. You know it, but more important, God knows it, and He isn't fooled by it. It would be the equivalent of handing a gun to a guy convicted of armed robbery and telling him to use it for good. So be sure to take a spiritual inventory of any sin blockages produced by pride in your life.

> *The advantage God's night vision provides for the fight is only as strong as the light your character maintains.*

Take a real close look. In fact, I hereby entreat all men to go back and look inside for any opposition to this message, and use *Risk* and *Dream* along with the workbooks to prepare for this fight. I know few readers will actually do it, but to look closely at your relationship to God's Word, its authority in your life, and how you are applying it in your relationships with people, you need the insights of *Every Man God's Man* and the first two books in the God's Man series, *Risk* and *Dream.* Let this serve as your warning.

The battle for godly thinking and character creates ambient spiritual light. And "light" means "usable night vision." The wisdom that creates our mismatch against the darkness begins with our personal commitment to wage war against light-draining sin, a willingness to let God illuminate it, and the follow-through to do whatever it takes to eliminate it.

You can check your ambient spiritual light by

*   asking God to show you any darkness in your life (see Psalm 139:23–24) and being willing to proactively deal with what He shows you
*   asking yourself if there is an area of your life you know is providing safe haven for darkness
*   asking your wife or close friend if either sees anything that produces a disconnect in your actions, character, and faith

Even with the best illumination and intelligence, there are still other hazards and unknowns coming into play as we get closer to the "knowledge targets" of our fight—a point not lost on my F-18 friend. There are other challenges to operating in the dark, even with night vision, that we must consider before launching into our intelligence briefing.

My buddy Paul vividly remembers his first night walking to his parked F-18 for his maiden flight with NVGs (night-vision goggles): "I remember thinking how dark it was, and while most Americans were tucking themselves in bed, I was about to ingress to a target in the desert traveling five hundred feet above ground level at over five hundred miles an hour." Going through his mind was the issue of having limited vision—no peripherals or depth perception, no more than a thirty-degree field of view. He'd trained for it, but it was still frightening. To take advantage of the technology, Paul would have to keep his head moving from side to side ("on a swivel") to get a picture of the threat. He also had to be aware of shadows, accumulated sand, or cloud cover playing tricks with the NVGs by hiding terrain in front of the plane. (Night-vision technology can make terrain appear like a canyon or a hole, and pilots can be tempted to fly through it—straight into the ground.) Finally, night vision is never complete without the most important night-ops tool—a wing man. "During night ops," Paul is quick to point out, "it's critical to have a wing man to check your 'six' [directly behind the aircraft] and process the threats as you get closer to a target, like surface-to-air missiles, triple-A fire, ground fire, and the ground itself."

As God's man you've been given the night vision you need to make this fight a mismatch, but you must learn to train with it and combine it with other disciplines to be successful. We see this admonition to combine godly character with godly information when the Scripture speaks to first-century Christians tormented under Roman persecution. Watch for how the tool and integration of its use are linked:

> His divine power has *given us everything we need* for life and godliness *through our knowledge of him* who called us by his own glory and goodness. Through these he has given us *his very great and precious promises,* so that through them you may participate in the divine nature and *escape the corruption in the world caused by evil desires.*
>
> For this very reason, *make every effort to add to your faith* goodness; and to goodness, knowledge; and to knowledge, self-control; and to self-control, perseverance; and to perseverance, godliness; and to godliness, brotherly kindness; and to brotherly kindness, love. For

if you possess these qualities in increasing measure, *they will keep you from being ineffective and unproductive in your knowledge of our Lord Jesus Christ.* (2 Peter 1:3–8)

The message is quite clear and quite sobering for our purposes: you can be God's man, be given evil-defeating authority, power, and knowledge, and still be ineffective and unproductive because of character issues. We must combine God's Word with inner disciplines to be effective against evil.

But perhaps of highest consequence for men in actively defeating evil is the "brotherly kindness" issue—their connection to other men. A wing man must be there. Whether under the canopy of an F-18 or in the life of God's man, the wing man is your lifeline, watching your six, putting eyes to your blind spots to help you process threats you can't even see. As the Scripture above reminds us, even with Satan-illuminating knowledge, you can fail if you don't employ the other tools. God says you need a wing man to win: "Though one may be overpowered, two can defend themselves" (Ecclesiastes 4:12). This is such a huge issue—the need for authentic male friendship and locking arms as brothers—and while I won't go into it here (pick up *Risk* and *Every Man God's Man* for essential insights), I will say that I've counseled too many leaders who didn't have a seasoned wing man checking their six.

Rule number one: never go into battle alone. Those who do so pay dearly for it. And worse still, most never recover. If you haven't found a brother to go through this book and the workbook with, find one and work it out together. There's really no other way. Dedication is useless without discernment, discernment is useless without a godly disposition, and godly disposition without a wing man illuminating your blind spots is pointless.

Heat Signatures

Actually, there's more than one way to see in the dark.

Some night-vision technology amplifies *heat.* My friend Paul calls these ground-mapping technologies FLIRS, which stands for Forward-Looking Infrared Sensors. On the ground, a soldier can hold a palm-size thermal imager that detects a particular object by sensing the difference between the heat radiated by the object and its surrounding environment. Since these thermal imagers do not rely on ambient light, they are uniquely independent of the need for light. This quality gives the FLIRS a penetrative capability that allows it to see through obstacles such as fog or battlefield smoke.

Satan emits his own forms of spiritual radiation, and it infects all his activities. In other words, he can't *not* emit heat! Our goal is not just knowledge of Satan but intuition about and awareness of his presence in and around us. But to have that, we have to get a *feel for him.* We need to know how his mind works, study his film, and learn his smell. He has certain methods he loves to employ that flow from a character that's not only predictable but preemptible.

The Scriptures form images for us through the dense fog and the clouding smoke of our emotions and misinformation. In the next chapter we will open the file on Satan himself. We'll make it our mission to know this enemy inside and out, to understand exactly why he acts as he does and why he cares so much about advancing on our territory. We'll look at his names and behaviors to get a good thermal image and combine the best *wisdom and knowledge* with our *intuition and senses* so we can have confidence in the fight. Our goal will be to ensure that we follow God's lead and His wisdom, as well as that of Gen. George S. Patton when commenting on his one *don't* in warfare: "Don't ever let the enemy pick the battle site."

The coming chapters in this section will cover and *uncover*

- Satan's terrorist cells, their goals, and their connections to you
- his moral and practical allies in the world
- his four main strategies and why they are effective but also highly predictable
- his fronts and covers that keep him unnoticed and actively destructive
- his unwitting human agents he uses against us
- his passionate love affair with religion
- and finally, his fears—and how he hates the stuff we do that ruins his plans

For now, the first enemy to slay is ignorance. And over the next few chapters we'll replace it with discernment. So let's get to it.

the arsonist: part one

Evil is comparatively harmless, feeble, and inert without the presence of its mighty inspirer.

—E. M. Bounds

In the book *Fire Lover,* Joseph Wambaugh takes you into the psyche of a man United States law enforcement publicly called the most prolific American arsonist of the twentieth century. It's a chilling, stranger-than-fiction portrait of a firefighter turned arsonist, shining the light on his crimes and his character. We learn his background and history that make sense of his crimes and acts of arson. Wambaugh's characterization of John Orr ignites, all at once, a deep loathing, a deep fear of fire, a deep compassion for the many victims, and a deep appreciation for the dogged trio of arson investigators who built the airtight case for Orr's arrest and ultimate conviction.

Mystified would be the best word to describe how arson investigators felt after experiencing the first waves of John Orr's devastating tapestry of flame in three separate cities in California. *Delusional* best describes the general reaction to salty arson investigator Marvin Casey's theory that the fires were the work of one of their own—an inside man. The only thing holding his idea together was a latent fingerprint from one of the crime scenes and an MO: yellow notebook paper, a cigarette butt, and three paper matches laid in foam pillows. Of course the fingerprint was run through law-enforcement databases without luck precisely because Orr was not a criminal. He was a well-disguised sociopath working for both law enforcement and arson investigation in the city of Glendale. The trail ran cold for years on these unsolved fires until a similar pattern began to emerge in the Los Angeles area, where three ATF agents had connected the dots and noted similarities to fires in central California. The MO matched. This led them to Bakersfield, where the inside-job theorist Marvin Casey lived. They brought home a fingerprint but were not hopeful.

They had the fingerprint enlarged and retraced graphically to sharpen the ridge lines before running it a second time. When they found a match in Los Angeles County law enforcement, they were incredulous. The print matched a rejected Los Angeles Police Academy candidate named John Orr, the current chief arson investigator for the city of Glendale. The bitter irony was only heightened by the fact that investigators all thought they knew John. Wasn't this guy a respected instructor and dedicated member of the fire and law-enforcement brotherhood?

Yes *and* no.

Desire, Scorn, and Fury

Believe it or not, John Orr had the benefit of the doubt when news of the fingerprint match hit the wire in law enforcement and fire authority circles. Even his battalion chief initially defended him. But as if putting together a jigsaw puzzle that looks overwhelming until you frame the edges, investigators were finding the straight-edged pieces of Orr's history that made the puzzle take shape.

The biggest of these pieces was his history with the LAPD or, perhaps more accurately, his *nonhistory.* The old file housing the right thumbprint that eventually linked Orr to the fires was the physical evidence that broke the case wide open. This, along with other hard evidence, answered the "who" question. Now investigators needed the "why." What was inside the man that drove him to go this far? What psychological need did the flames meet that nothing else could? What did the fires really represent for Orr? How did the man become the monster who ceased having a conscience? What made him evil?

The answer was in the file.

After John Orr aced his written exams for entrance into the LAPD, he could taste his fantasy of a law-enforcement career coming true. When called in for his final interview, there was that positive expectation and confidence a man feels when he senses he's nailed it. So when the interviewer told John that his application was being rejected based on his psychological exam, the encounter progressed from excitement to disorientation to shock. With his file open, the interviewer calmly explained that John would never become an LAPD officer and then excused himself, leaving John's file lying tantalizingly (seemingly purposefully) in front of him. For a man searching for an answer, that temptation was irresistible. John read the file, and one word leaped off the page: "unsuitable."

And so a monster was conceived.

That one word captures the ten-megaton explosion of a man's pride and the obliteration of a dream. It would be the acid rain on his parade every time he was promoted and recognized by the Glendale Fire Department. It would be the source of insatiable hunger for prominence and recognition in his field. It would form the passive-aggressive mentality that would make him unnoticeable and lethal. It would be the source of an inner grudge too deep to be predicted or understood. It would be the humongous chip on his shoulder no one would ever see, the demon that would possess him and control him to the end.

In reconstructing John Orr, we see a man who never wanted to be a fireman or an arson investigator. We see a man whose desire for power, position, control, and respect was intimately connected to a badge and a gun—two things he would never legitimately possess. The once-convoluted and confusing jigsaw puzzle of a good guy turned serial arsonist gets filled in, and the shapes and shadows show a picture almost too grisly to be believed.

John Orr did not choose the world inhabited by firemen. He was banished there by the LAPD. We see that the prolific arsonist whom Orr became was created and energized by a painful rejection that his mind, heart, and character could never accept. And rather than sating his need for authority and superiority, advancement in the fire department only made that need stronger. His identity now, literally, had to rise from the ashes. The most wounding rejection became the source of his psychological transformation. The severity of the wound provided the clarity of his new purpose.

> *The most wounding rejection became the source of his psychological transformation.*

From here, we can see a little of John Orr in ourselves. Anger provides both clarity and confusion: clarity of purpose and confusion in our conscience telling us not to do those very same things. When a man wants something badly enough and is angry enough, *he doesn't want to think.* Our appetite for "justice" takes over, and we go from stupid to enslaved. All creatures of free will are subject to these forces. John Orr was no exception. His emotional profile and professional free fall formed a pool of deadly accelerant simply waiting for a spark. And that moment arrived upon his approval by and acceptance into the fledgling Glendale Fire Department.

Although Orr was a fireman, he would not let go of his ambition to be accepted and acknowledged as a cop. Like any number of fictional or mythological characters, Orr's ambitions matched with his psychological issues to create a savvy manipulator and a politico able to meet his need in whichever framework he found himself:

- He found a way to carry a firearm on duty.
- On his off time he would stake out, catch, capture, and report adolescent fire-starters to the police.
- He "found himself" in the midst of multiple situations acting as a police officer and collaring crime suspects to the dismay of legitimate law enforcement, often stealing headlines and "saving the day."
- He used his growing authority as fire captain and eventually chief arson investigator to integrate law-enforcement capacities into his job description.
- He drove a Crown Victoria and outfitted it with sirens and portable emergency lights.
- When examined upon arrest, his badge had a removable secondary nameplate inscribed "Police Officer."

Can you say "pathetic"? This is what Orr had become: insecure, weak, and pitiable in the eyes of law enforcement. But when you combine these character defects with power, position, intelligence, and a deep grudge, the result is nearly unstoppable. Never fully accepted by law enforcement, made fun of as a wannabe, and now driven by a need to feel superior, Orr's legal means of achieving his dream were exhausted. But what the fire profession could never provide, the flames could. His lust for recognition overrode all reason, and Orr started lighting fires to become infamous. From his position as chief arson investigator, he projected an image of authority, had access and control over the flow of information and unlimited mobility, and could be expected in or around the scene of any fire.

Because he positioned himself as a good guy, practicing evil was never this easy. And yet Orr's greatest security was his forgettable persona. "Everybody who knew John Orr always said how ordinary he looked, the kind of guy nobody ever notices. The kind that blends into whatever background there is and just disappears."[1] His greatest strength as an arsonist was his ability to remain incognito.

The unfathomable toll of Orr's exploits defies all logic when pinning the devastation to its point of origin: *one man with a grudge, a lust to gain respect, and a match.* What's more, the lost homes, lost businesses, lost jobs, lost acreage, and lost lives pale in comparison to the widespread emotional toll. And yet, psychologically, these were the exact results that produced a chemical high for Orr, the wannabe cop. A man's ego dwarfed by rejection creates an inflated ego bent on possessing and controlling those he despises.

Sound familiar?

Being told you're unsuitable and finding yourself excluded can breed a unique, visceral, and deadly hostility from which men *and* fallen angels find it hard to recover.

The Wannabe God

The Bible contains the file on Satan. In it we find what we need to know about him, his history, his failures, his abilities, his plans, and his intentions toward us. The first step in discerning evil is to understand that Satan is a living personality with a complex depth of character. He has an inner life that informs his actions and shapes his existence. He also has a past. To discern him, we must get intimate with his personality and how it was formed. He certainly has a reputation, but that comes from his character.

What formed his character is right there in his file. As with Orr's rejection after a failed psychological exam, there was something inside Satan that God's holiness couldn't accept. Something wasn't right. There was a flaw, an unhealthy fondness for the power of his position, that turned him self-serving. God sensed it and responded in a manner consistent with His character, banishing Satan from heaven:

> You were anointed as a guardian cherub,
>> for so I ordained you.
> You were on the holy mount of God;
>> you walked among the fiery stones.
> You were blameless in your ways
>> from the day you were created
>> till wickedness was found in you.
> Through your widespread trade
>> you were filled with violence,
>> and you sinned.
> So I drove you in disgrace from the mount of God,
>> and I expelled you, O guardian cherub,
>> from among the fiery stones.

Your heart became proud
>> on account of your beauty,
and you corrupted your wisdom
>> because of your splendor.
So I threw you to the earth;
>> I made a spectacle of you before kings.
By your many sins and dishonest trade
>> you have desecrated your sanctuaries.
So I made a fire come out from you,
>> and it consumed you,
and I reduced you to ashes on the ground
>> in the sight of all who were watching. (Ezekiel 28:14–18)

Satan was created by God and employed in His service. He stood between God and the praise that was offered. His merchandise was worship. Passing through his hands were the authority and dominion of God above him and the returned worship of created beings below him. He was a trusted employee, a senior manager, and the most articulate spokesman ever created. Then he *attached.*

He attached to himself some of the worship he was supposed to pass along to God. He attached to himself some of the authority that belonged to God alone. He attached to himself the orders God was giving and hijacked them, wanting some of his own under his own authority. He grew attached to his beauty, magnificence, and power and felt entitled to receive a little adulation for himself. Satan decided to embezzle God's glory. So here in the file, we find the origin of all evil, the genesis of sin, the first opposition to God, and God's subsequent response. There is only one will in heaven, and Satan tried to introduce a second one—his. He attached to himself and took for himself what was not his. This made him "unsuitable," and God ensured that heaven would not be polluted by his character.

The similarities between Orr and Lucifer are shared because they're inspired by the shared misery:

- A character issue was spotted and exposed.
- Dreams of power, control, and authority were unrealized.
- Pride was wounded profoundly.
- Punishment was permanent separation from the world he wanted to rule.
- Stripped of power, he was humiliated.
- Appetites grew from the desire to be somebody.
- Brooding emotions overflowed when opportunity presented itself.

Satan was permanently banned from the job he loved, cast out and sent to a dark, formless, and vacuous earth void of life. For how long, no one knows, but Satan was imprisoned here on earth before there was life in that interval between Genesis 1:2 and 1:3. He was master of nothing, with lots of time for his anger to fester. Like Orr, he was a pool of accelerant just waiting for the spark, that moment when the lights were unexpectedly turned on in Genesis 1:3: "God said, 'Let there be light.'" If there is such a thing as evil joy, Satan gave it its first expression. Suddenly, he had a place to let out all his frustration and the sinister intent toward God that had been stored up in him.

Satan was a creature on fire.

You Must Get This

You and I are living in the next act of this unfolding story. In creating man, God gave Satan an object on which to project his latent hostility toward God. The sufferings and agonies that have flowed from that moment lead us to the ultimate question we must resolve: *Why didn't God deal with Satan before allowing him to set the world on fire and create so much pain?* If you're like me, you can't look at the Holocaust, the genocide in Rwanda, 9/11, or myriad other senseless evils throughout history and *not* ask this question. And if you're like me, you might have a hard time getting your arms around the answer.

In fact, *we* are the reason He didn't nuke Satan from the get-go. It's not that He couldn't. It's because there were larger considerations. One of them was us—His future sons. In this time between one eternity and the next comes the age of men and the battle against evil on earth. It seems

> *We are the reason He didn't nuke Satan from the get-go.*

like a long time, but it's not, sandwiched as it is between the two halves of forever. Had God obliterated Satan, He could never have created another being as magnificent as Lucifer, able to be seated with God in heaven, possessing a will to worship but never a will to rebel. That other creation is *you.* God is permitting evil to have limited success now so that out of this age will come sons who are able to share His glory but not *attach to it* like Satan did. These sons, the Bible teaches,

- will rule with God from a position higher than that of the angels
- will have prominence and dignity far exceeding Lucifer's
- will hold powers higher than Satan's
- will never ponder rebellion against God

In other words, because of the creation and fall of man, the appearance and atoning death of Jesus Christ, and the new nature implanted in every believer who has trusted Christ for salvation, *sin will never break out again in heaven.* My personal life verses (the one passage of the Bible that

I feel describes my story) reflect on the reason this is a fact now as well as portending the future. It is bracketed in my Bible and reads

> I waited patiently for the LORD;
>> he turned to me and heard my cry.
> He lifted me out of the slimy pit,
>> out of the mud and mire;
> he set my feet on a rock
>> and gave me a firm place to stand.
> He put a new song in my mouth,
>> a hymn of praise to our God.
> Many will see and fear
>> and put their trust in the LORD. (Psalm 40:1–3)

Sentimentality aside, no man rescued from the slimy pit of his own sin and given this kind of traction and prominence will *ever* desire to take the glory for his own. Instead, he'll give the glory back. God's plan is to replace the lost hosts of heaven with a new class of creation, a higher class of creation with a higher view of God and a lower, more humble view of itself. This new creation, sons, will be governing the universe with Him and gladly passing along all the glory to Him. *There will never be another rebellion in heaven because you will be there to make sure there isn't.* Satan gets the fullest opportunity possible to exploit every aspect of his power upon earth so that, in the end, God can prove that any created thing's will in conflict with His own is doomed to fail.

This is the big picture.

The reason I bring this up in our discussion of discerning evil and the need to understand Satan intimately is this: *you are his replacement.* You must get this. Not only does he know this, he loathes this with every fiber of his being. He loathes *you*. He was deemed unsuitable and replaced with a redeemed sinner who has been made a son. This makes his blood boil. This is *the* issue. The big jigsaw puzzle called evil begins to find its shape and context *here*.

So now that we have the outline, we need to fill out our portrait of this organized Serial Arsonist.

the arsonist: part two

One pack of Camel cigarettes
One cigarette lighter
One plastic bag of rubber bands
Two books of matches
One pair of small binoculars
  —Items found in the trunk of John Orr's car by investigators

When arson investigators in Los Angeles were baffled by a string of unsolved fires in retail districts and locations, the only solid pieces of evidence linking the fires were the incendiary devices used to start them. In some locations the fires were discovered and extinguished before they could spread and cause damage. These cases preserved the evidence. But even in the ashes of larger fires, arson investigators were able to find the remnants of the same incendiary device. Whoever the arsonist was, he thought his starters would be untraceable in the fire. But the common denominators in all of them were a cigarette, three paper matches, and a rubber band. It was something, but investigators could do little with the evidence until they actually found these items in a suspect's possession.

And the chances of that were one in a million. Despite investigating all possible leads and motives, they were still light-years from solving the mystery.

After John Orr's fingerprint was matched, a case was built over months of searching. A warrant was obtained, they popped the trunk of his car, and to no one's surprise they found the items. No one actually saw John Orr light a cigarette, bundle matches around it, or place them in any location. But he was eventually tried and convicted by a mountain of circumstantial evidence pointing directly to him:

- the fingerprint from the store in central California
- repeated eyewitness identification of photo number five (Orr's) as the man they saw at the scene
- store employee accounts of Orr visiting establishments five to six times before the fires
- his presence at arson investigator conventions close to the dates in the regions where fires occurred
- his novel he was trying to get published called *Points of Origin,* detailing a firefighter/arsonist beginning an arson spree that, irony of ironies, amazingly paralleled Orr's crimes
- the contents in the trunk of his car
- the fact that Orr was not a smoker

Jurors convicted and sentenced John Orr to life in prison, and investigators claimed he was responsible for as many as two thousand fires—over twelve million dollars in property damage, the destruction of thousands of acres of forest, and numerous deaths.

The jury did not need video of him striking a match. They knew he was there. He was guilty based on the evidence.

The case is fortunate but rare. Wambaugh told a CNN reporter that serial arsonists are seldom caught. "He's the most difficult of all serial offenders to catch. He doesn't brag about his crimes. He uses fast escapes and pretty well keeps to himself. And it is thrill-motivated, so he very well could be there watching the fire."[1] Orr could easily have escaped but for the one fingerprint connecting all the dots. The thing about finger-prints is that they usually only get there if the criminal puts them there.

Satan Exposed

Pinning Satan is easier than catching a serial arsonist. He leaves the clean prints of his character and presence wherever he's been. So why, after Jesus' powerful work at the cross, the sending and indwelling of the Holy Spirit, the clear teaching about him by Jesus and Scripture, and the rapid spread of the gospel worldwide, have Satan's victories over God's people enjoyed such an incredible run?

The first part of the answer has to do with Satan's potent skills. He's the master of redirecting suspicions about the points of origin and the person of origin *away from himself* and onto others, onto circumstances, onto organizations, churches, bad doctrine, anything else but the *real* source. The second part of the answer lies with us and our indifference toward his person, abilities, and designs upon us. Indifference is synonymous with ignorance, and ignorance is synonymous with defeat. That's why he's embarrassingly successful against God's people—functional knowl-edge undiligently applied. God Himself says that ruin closely follows a lack of awareness: "My people are destroyed from lack of knowledge" (Hosea 4:6). Satan likes it that way.

In contrast, God's man, in the character of his Lord, is called to see what others cannot. When others see only circumstances or people, we're called to deploy our spiritual intuition, dust for prints, look at things from a different angle, shine the light in unusual places, and ask deeper questions based on our knowledge of the seething Arsonist. We should be able to sense his character leaking into everyday situations. We may not see him strike the match, but we know the fires he likes to set, how he likes to set them, what he uses to set them, and even how he entices us to hold and strike the match for him!

He's played us all at one time or another, and he's relentless at exerting his influence in every way he can. In relationships, in morals, in spiritually illuminating moments, and in emotional experiences, he's always involved. The reason is that these are where he gains the most: in the basic transactions of your soul. But knowing this in advance diminishes the chances that he can play you or manipulate you.

> *To catch the Great Arsonist, the spiritually aware God's man must make the causal connections.*

Of course, just knowing this isn't enough. You must know *him*—his character and the ways it manifests in his conduct. When you see certain dynamics happening in people or situations, those reflect particular clues about their source. To catch the Great Arsonist, the spiritually aware God's man must make the causal connections.

Jesus didn't hesitate to out Satan when His radar picked up Satan's telltale qualities. He knew: "That's Satan!" His radar squawked and blinked red for a number of reasons. If we look carefully, we can get a picture of the unrepentantly evil character we're dealing with. Watch and learn from the Master. And remember, *He is the God-Man who lives in you.* Here is what He had to say about Satan:

- *He has murderous intent.* " 'If you were Abraham's children,' said Jesus, 'then you would do the things Abraham did. As it is, you are determined to kill me, a man who has told you the truth that I heard from God. Abraham did not do such things. You are doing the things your own father does' " (John 8:39–41).

  Translation: "This is coming from the Great Murderer. You guys are under the influence: DUI, the Devil's Urging and Influence."

- *He lies and deceives to justify evil actions.* "You belong to your father, the devil, and you want to carry out your father's desire. He was a murderer from the beginning, not holding to the truth, for there is no truth in him. When he lies, he speaks his native language, for he is a liar and the father of lies" (John 8:44).

  Translation: "It's not about you. It's your lips and body, but it's the Devil. Rational lies means the Liar is involved here."

- *He practices self-interest and self-gratification at others' expense.* "The thief comes only to steal and kill and destroy; I have come that they may have life, and have it to the full. I am the good shepherd. The good shepherd lays down his life for the sheep. The hired hand is not the shepherd who owns the sheep. So when he sees the wolf coming, he abandons the sheep and runs away. Then the wolf attacks the flock and scatters it. The man runs away because he is a hired hand and cares nothing for the sheep" (John 10:10–13).

  Translation: "He's not in it for you! He's into you for him! Satan coined the term, 'What's in it for me?' His pride led to a spirit of entitlement and self-interest. He's a pimp. Stick with the Good Shepherd and not the guy who promises pleasure but delivers pain. See people being used? That's him."

- *He uses mental diversion and distraction to eliminate spiritual transformation.* "The seed is the word of God. Those along the path are the ones who hear, and then the devil comes and takes away the word from their hearts, so that they may not believe and be saved" (Luke 8:11–12).

Translation: "When distraction and diversions come before you read the Word or go to church, watch for the Terrorist. When there's potential for a truth encounter, Satan works to discourage it. It may seem like justifiable disinterest, but make no mistake, it's him."

- *He uses many words to mask his lack of integrity.* "But I tell you, Do not swear at all: either by heaven, for it is God's throne; or by the earth, for it is his footstool; or by Jerusalem, for it is the city of the Great King. And do not swear by your head, for you cannot make even one hair white or black. Simply let your 'Yes' be 'Yes,' and your 'No,' 'No'; anything beyond this comes from the evil one" (Matthew 5:34–37).

  Translation: "Satan is the Great Salesman. He'll say anything to get you to bite. When people try to convince you of something using lots of words, something's up. Satan invented this trick."

- *He hijacks God's plan through man's passions and self-interest.* "From that time on Jesus began to explain to his disciples that he must go to Jerusalem and suffer many things at the hands of the elders, chief priests and teachers of the law, and that he must be killed and on the third day be raised to life. Peter took him aside and began to rebuke him. 'Never, Lord!' he said. 'This shall never happen to you!' Jesus turned and said to Peter, 'Get behind me, Satan! You are a stumbling block to me; you do not have in mind the things of God, but the things of men'" (Matthew 16:21–23).

  Translation: "Satan loves that men desire comfort and choose it over sacrifice. He'll tempt you by suggesting a more comfortable way, but God demands uncomfortable sacrifices. When someone comes offering an easier way, often Satan has a hand up his back. Beware the puppet and the Puppeteer."

- *He opposes the advance of the gospel in one's life.* "The proconsul, an intelligent man, sent for Barnabas and Saul because he wanted to hear the word of God. But Elymas the sorcerer (for that is what his name means) opposed them and tried to turn the proconsul from the faith. Then Saul, who was also called Paul, filled with the Holy Spirit, looked straight at Elymas and said, 'You are a child of the devil and an enemy of everything that is right! You are full of all kinds of deceit and trickery. Will you never stop perverting the right ways of the Lord? Now the hand of the Lord is against you. You are going to be blind, and for a time you will be unable to see the light of the sun'" (Acts 13:7–11).

    Translation: "See opposition to the gospel? That's Satan. Deception? Bet on his involvement. Trickery and manipulation? He's got a hand in that too. Right being twisted into wrong? You get the picture."

When I see Paul and Barnabas acting so confidently, I see Jesus continuing to live through them, unmasking the Devil. Then I ask, "Where are the men doing this today?" I look around at the men in my church, and I'm convicted to more diligently train them to see Satan. It's not a Kenny thing. It's way bigger than that. It's a Jesus thing. Jesus said the whole goal is to be good at this stuff because it means we're becoming like Him. "Everyone who is fully trained will be like his teacher" (Luke 6:40). Key words: *fully trained.*

Satan hates to be seen. Jesus knew this. That's why He never

> **fight fact**
> *When God's man sees the character of Satan and distinguishes between the manipulator and the person being manipulated, it is a huge blow to Satan's work.*

entered situations with His radar turned off. He knew Satan would always show up one way or another, and He viewed Himself and His disciples as shepherds to sheep among wolves. The wolves would be ever present. He spoke of the wheat (us) growing right next to the weeds, explaining that it would be that way until He came again (see Matthew 13:37–39). In this "not yet time" before the future begins, God's men are working, living, and engaging others who are under the direct control and influence of Satan. The way Jesus met them was by first *knowing Satan's character and how it manifested,* and then by simply *calling him out.* Being familiar with Satan as a living being with a personality and character that are both recognizable and confrontable is the name of the game.

More from the File

Satan's rap sheet stretches for miles. I've only scratched the surface of his character and manifestations. I cannot stress enough how God's man must read the Word with a lens for both spiritual application and fortification against the Enemy. We have to study and analyze with care every mention and appearance of Satan as well as his victories and defeats detailed in Scripture.

In the most sinister way, all his character qualities become the methods he uses to kill. Discerning *him* leads us to discern what he's doing. His behavior always reflects his character. So let's look at a few more synonyms for Satan. When you see these in your circumstances, you can bank on his involvement at every level.

He's Synonymous with Pride

The language of pride is "I know better." It has multiple forms including all types of narcissism, self-promotion, defensiveness, arrogance, and entitlement. All of these separate people from God because they make people their own god, violating the first commandment and estranging them from their Creator. Think about Satan's own story. His pride begets entitlement, which begets embezzlement of God's glory. You could say the first sin was pride in Satan's heart. "My kingdom, my power, my glory" is his anthem, and he loves a chorus.

He's Synonymous with Death

He is the original serial killer, and he is after more than stopping hearts. If homicide, suicide, or killing children is out of reach or ineffective, he will work to kill relationships, marriages, and families so that they will wipe out the next generation without more effort on his part. Abortion, yes, but divorce is just as good.

Satan Is Synonymous with Rebellion

He's a rebel with a cause. Follow the disintegration of the family and God's commandment to children to honor their parents. Parents who rebel against God's authority over their lives will parent children who see the hypocrisy and in turn rebel against their parents' authority. Are we surprised by this? It all starts with creating an environment of respect and modeling it in the home. Children who don't learn to respect authority will struggle to respect God. Rebellion is the name of Satan's game.

He Is Synonymous with Out-of-Control Appetites

Lives ruled by a fix, a meal, an adrenaline hit, a relationship, a purchase, a bet, a business deal, a porn site, or another immediate pleasure are easy to manage and destroy. These people are horrible at relationships because they've met their need for comfort by feeding a surrogate appetite. Their idols fulfill their need to worship, and they become enslaved. The "why" is inconsequential.

Satan Is Synonymous with Relational Separation

Satan is a lonely creature, has no friends, and is completely devoid of love. So he projects his own loneliness and misery upon people by attacking their connections to God and others. *Satan can't stand healthy, connected relationships inhabited by healthy people who are growing in God.* That's why relationship experts tracking connections report 55 percent of all marriages end in divorce, and 40 percent of all Christian marriages are touched by infidelity within the first ten years. That's why fatherlessness is linked to a quadrupling of drug use, incarceration, teen pregnancy, and high-school dropout rates.[2] Separating and isolating people can make them easy to destroy.

Satan Is Synonymous with the Magnification of Negative Emotions

Because we are what we think and do what we think, Satan loves to play with negative emotions by magnifying them. His goal is for you to agree 110 percent with whatever you are feeling. We engage his suggestions and escalate our emotions, then they enslave our minds, leading to actions that help us hang ourselves. He is the crown prince of suggestions, and his timing is impeccable. They will come when your emotions are at a fever pitch, because it's at those moments when your desire to think is low and your desire to act on your emotions is high. He knows that when we want, we don't want to think.

> *His goal is for you to agree 110 percent with whatever you are feeling.*

He Is Synonymous with a Hurried Pace of Life

Satan knows that "quick and quality" is an oxymoron. Key word: *moron.* Only a moron says that you can have quality relationships with God or people on the fly. Instead of living your life from a set of God-ordered values, you find that Satan encourages the activity-driven life versus the purpose-driven every time. He says success isn't living out your values, it's maintaining your image and making sure you're a part of all the urgent matters you have to get to.

I'm saving a few of the biggies for later, but you get the point. The Bible tells us that believers are at risk of being bamboozled by Satan's masks. He projects his character onto you by planting thoughts that sound positive but produce devastating effects. Search out his file and study it so you won't lack the wisdom and intuition to see him.

"We need the knowledge about the enemy, his character, presence, and power in order to arouse men to action," echoes E. M. Bounds. "This knowledge is vital to victory."[3] If God's man is destroyed from lack of knowledge (see Hosea 4:6), then God's man who is equipped with intimate knowledge of the Enemy will do some damage of his own.

A fighting God's man must begin by being dedicated to discerning the Devil. The Bible *assumes* Satan's clear and dangerous presence in the affairs of men and reveals his person and character so that we can nail him. This is our training and our calling.

Remember, you are shortly going to replace him in heaven forever. *Clear linkage is the key.* Just as investigators made a causal link from the evidence in John Orr's trunk, God's man can look at Satan's character within God's Word to grow a deeper awareness. Like a fully trained special-op fighter, we will catch the Intruder's scent and expose and rebuke him in the name of Christ.

His file is there for us to use. Commit it to memory, and apply it every day to preempt him.

Our motto: Incognito no more.

assassins on assignment

He was the perfect soldier: he went where you sent him,
stayed where you put him, and had no idea of his own to keep
him from doing exactly what you told him.
                              —DASHIELL HAMMETT

I was working across the street from the happiest place on earth—Disney-
land, for the uninitiated. I was a chaplain in an oncology unit on the
seventh floor of Western Medical Center in Anaheim, California. The
irony of working so close to Fantasyland was that my world, filled with
the reality of mortality, was juxtaposed to a world designed specifically
to drown out that reality. Things always worked out over in the Magic
Kingdom. A hero for every crisis, and menacing evil *always* lost.

But high up in my castle of sterility across the freeway, I would pray to
God, asking for His wisdom and strength to help many patients face the
fact that their fantasies of being cancer free were exactly that and that
their days were numbered. Many patients went to great lengths to find a

cure for their cancers. They searched in vain for some new therapy, some undiscovered magic bullet lethal enough to kill their particular cancer.

That kind of ammunition proved elusive, and most patients had to settle for conventional therapies that were risky and came with huge side effects. In most cases, doctors had to nearly kill a patient (or at least an immune system) to kill the cancer. Poison and radiation are counterintuitive healing agents, no matter how you slice it. Dimmer still is the painful journey for patients and loved ones praying and hoping for a good outcome.

Often the aggressiveness and pace of the cancers eclipsed the discovery of new therapies to defeat them. But one day up on that seventh floor I learned that magic bullets aren't always the realm of fantasy.

I first heard of monoclonal antibodies (MABs) from my director of oncology, Marianne Gonsalvez. We were talking during case management about our patients, their different types of cancers, and what was being done to help them. As she explained what MABs do inside the human body, my jaw dropped. For lack of a better image, these are the bioengineered cruise missiles that fly past every other type of cell and target only the cancer cells. Excitedly, Marianne further explained that when a monoclonal antibody attached to a cancer cell, it would

- highlight a cancer cell to the immune system. Like a homing beacon, the MABs can tag cancerous cells for the immune system, making them easier to locate and fight.
- impede growth signals. Think radar jamming. Certain cancer cells are signaled to grow faster than normal cells. MABs can be programmed to jam and confuse those signals.

- deliver radiation. Think kamikazes. An MAB can carry a radioactive particle directly to the target cancer cell, sparing the surrounding healthy cells. Once the MAB attaches to a receptor on a cancer cell, it delivers its payload at the site of the rogue cell.
- smuggle drugs *into* a cancer cell. Like a Trojan horse, the MAB can introduce drugs to the cancer cell, remaining inactive until *inside* the cell. Once through, the drug can be activated, killing the cancer in a biologically sublime bait and switch.

Two types of leukemia, four types of cancer, and non-Hodgkin's lymphoma are regularly treated today with monoclonal antibodies. They

> *Demons are his personal assassins on assignment, and as far as he is concerned, we are the cancer.*

are truly the magic bullets of cancer therapy. This picture of the intentional targeting and destruction of cancer cells is as mysterious as it is inspiring.

They are the perfect soldiers of the oncology world:

- going where you send them
- staying where you put them
- doing exactly what the bioengineer tells them to do
- targeting defects in cancer cells and exploiting them
- existing for one purpose
- carrying highly lethal capability
- representing the highest intentions of the doctor as his agent of eradication

Combine all those, and you begin to see why MABs are the treatment of choice for cancer: disease specific, positionable, and lethal to cancer, yet

> ## fight fact
> *Demons are constantly seeking to attach themselves to the lives of believers in areas that are unsurrendered to the Holy Spirit's control. The flesh and the world are able to control God's man, and demons have the same potential. God's man must recognize this as a practical and personal reality and take steps to defend against, rebuke, and resist their presence and purposes.*

benign to healthy cells. There are obvious connotations here for God's men as agents of the kingdom. Similarly for Satan, his demons provide his ability to strike intimately and fatally with laserlike precision all over the world. They are his personal assassins on assignment, and as far as he is concerned, *we are the cancer.*

Murderous Angelic Beings (MABs)

Just as cancer cells unwittingly cooperate with monoclonal antibodies, resulting in their own destruction, God's men have unwittingly cooperated with demons and been the target of their attacks since the creation of man. In the New Testament, Judas was both tempted away from the inner circle and possessed by Satan, and he was later overwhelmed by guilt, driving him to suicide. Peter was influenced and persuaded to try to talk Jesus out of going to the cross. After that, he went from faithful disciple to a curser and a liar who felt so defiled that he crawled under a rock and tried to forget his identity as God's man. It took a real-life "come to Jesus" meeting to reel him back in. Also, John and James wanted to call down fire on the Samaritans in Luke 9, and Jesus rebuked them for possessing a spirit other than His. The prevailing motives of their hearts were being exploited by another influence. Satan and his MABs were on the attack, attaching and delivering their evil.

Demons are murderous angelic beings on assignment and under orders from Satan himself. They have a file too in the Word of God. The Scripture teaches us what we need to know about these perfect soldiers of Satan. Here are the basics every God's man should know about Satan's MABs:

- They have great personal power and passion.
- They are ordered, subordered, and coordinated within a hierarchy of power, with Satan at the top of the food chain.
- They are numerous and everywhere in the world, projecting and promoting evil influences and actions.
- They exist to target both believers and nonbelievers with malice and destructive intent.
- They attach themselves to a believer's life, seeking to control whatever area is *not* under the control and leadership of the Holy Spirit. *(Think about that one for a second.)*
- They are highly intelligent agents, intimate with Satan and emotionally close to him by virtue of their shared histories, miseries, and destinies.
- They are militarily minded and exist to conquer men, cultures, nations, and the church in order to increase Satan's control.
- They are given permission by believers to influence, control, and oppress them by compromising or compartmentalizing areas of life away from Christ's control.
- They have no authority or control over a believer who is in fellowship with the Holy Spirit.
- They are the ones we should be concerned about in our quest to be God's men and fulfill His purposes on earth.

One other thing—you can't "sort of" believe in demons as God's man. "For our struggle is not against flesh and blood, but against the rulers, against the authorities, against the powers of this dark world and against the spiritual forces of evil in the heavenly realms" (Ephesians 6:12). We give this verse a lot of lip service but little practical action. In fact, there's woefully little actual resistance to demonic influence and control in the lives of God's men today. We are being forked over to them through mental compartmentalization and compromise.

> *One other thing—you can't "sort of" believe in demons as God's man.*

You can go ahead and think I'm off base, but I want to make sure we all get this burned on our brains: spiritual compartmentalization in our lifestyles—whether 5 percent or 95—ensures demonic presence and influence in our lives. Demons work overtime to ensure that the unsurrendered parts of our lives take down the whole thing. They love turning dabbling in sin into full-scale disasters and death. I have a stack of e-mails in my office from our brothers in Christ to prove it.

What we need to understand about all this effort on evil's part is that Satan tries to parody and imitate God's work in a perverted way. When God creates man and seeks to lead him, love him, and bless him, Satan gets in on the act, promising the same things but delivering pain. When God becomes incarnate in the person of Jesus Christ, Satan uses demons to take forcible possession of people and become pseudoincarnate himself. When Jesus Christ resurrects from the dead and the Holy Spirit comes to permanently and rightfully dwell in believers, Satan, using his MABs, seeks an ongoing and artificial presence in the lives of believers.

Instead of feeling the fellowship and agreement of the Holy Spirit, we sense the unnatural and contradictory feelings of an intruder. Demons are like terrorists attempting to nest in a foreign land—they are unwelcomed but present. They can reside in those permitted spaces of a believer's life with a destructive mission. They cannot indwell as the Holy Spirit does because that is neither their mission nor their legal right. They will, however, attempt to seize areas where there exists the smallest openness to entertain a will other than God's. They want to drive the boat in that particular area of a life, have a voice, get a yes, explode a bomb, maim, kill, and move on to their next host community.

Demons are patient and persistent in their quest to gradually insinuate their influence on your thinking to gain control of a piece of your life. They will work against you just as your flesh and the world will. They will encourage gray areas and complaints about discomfort or loss, and then they offer easy solutions. They will exploit your conflictedness and pounce on negative emotions with a laundry list of suggestions provided by Satan himself. They will help arrange your thinking in such a way so that sin looks *really* good and totally logical. They like to intrude and invade your life with *a lot* of bad thinking. These guys are not from the neighborhood. They are salesmen who have been studying your film. They know the character of men and exactly what to play to among our frailties, pride, and insecurities. They've learned from the master. They are on your porch because they smell disagreement and rebellion in your spirit, like bloody chum in the water attracts a school of sharks.

You know it's Satan and his murderous angelic beings when the suggestions, thoughts, fears, discouragements, temptations, and core conflicts are getting magnified in your imagination. Then there will be an offering of a reality that's better than any God is offering. It's not just a solution; it's a *voluptuous* solution—one that plays into your feelings and overrides your faith. Multiple millions of these battles are being waged right this second in the lives of people all over the world. There are no cease-fires, no lulls, no moments of relaxation, and no truces. The reason is that the ever-present flaws in your character can produce conflicts that damage your relationships with God and people.

It is unceasing because we are in *their backyard,* and not vice versa. Earth is in a fallen condition where fallen angelic beings have been given power to rule over and dominate nations and men. We are in that world, and those who rule it in this short time between eternities can't stand to give up a single inch of control.

Control is their deadly game, and they have great experience with the male personality and its frailties and insecurities, which helps them achieve their ends. It's this intelligence, teamwork, and relentlessness in achieving the self-destruction of men that causes us to scratch our heads when we see men morph into people we don't recognize. They go from ordinary guys to obnoxious, immoral, malicious, worldly, self-serving, or worse. Believer or unbeliever, the greatest weakness a man can have is being unaware that he has given access to a demon, because it's that blindness that will do him in.

From Average to Evil

As a little boy in Egypt, Mohamed Atta was not a threat. He was the son of a lawyer and played chess, and his nickname in Arabic meant "singing little bird." In the family, success cast some long shadows over his life with his older sisters becoming a doctor and a university professor respectively.

At Cairo University, Atta's classmates described him as a bit of a loner and never saw him pray, and when pressed, Atta called Islamic terrorists "brainless." His best friend during that time said, "He was not a leader. He had his opinion, but he was modest in everything. His emotions were steady, and he was not easily influenced or swayed.... He never offended or bothered anyone."[1]

The more I read about this guy, the more I got the sense that he wanted to be "for" something. His friends in college talked about a young man who would be quiet and reserved most of the time, and then certain things would trigger an angst leading to an explosion of random convictions about weird stuff. Atta would explode suddenly about things ranging from injustice in the world to the death of an insect to the irritating behaviors of a classmate. You might have called it "little man syndrome." You know these guys, with so little stature and purpose that they become angry at what they have become, and there's no foreseeable way to be more than what they have become.

Upon graduation from the university, there was a deep fear in Mohamed Atta that he wouldn't make it professionally in his own country. The academic system was against him, the politics of his profession were against him, and his prospects were consequently dim. You could say that he was struggling to make his mark as a man. Somewhere along the line this guy's manhood had been broken. In graduate school in Germany it got worse. Atta went from just being cynical to being sullen to being depressed. He felt more like a professional student than a man—no family, no career, and nothing tangible to point to after investing all those years in school. Then, to the surprise of his fellow graduate students and teachers, Mohamed Atta started disappearing for long spans of time, taking trips to the Middle East. When he came back to Germany, his appearance changed from clean-cut to having a bushy beard.

The next time Atta surfaced at school in Germany it was to seek permission to start an Islamic student group on campus. Suddenly he and more than forty classmates were gathering for daily prayers, two of whom ended up also becoming hijackers. He had found something powerful: an identity and a purpose. He had gone from having little to say to having a lot to say, and from marginally Muslim to devout and evangelistic.

The rest of Atta's transformation is now very public and very evil. He dropped the beard, came to the United States, and began training for and planning the 9/11 attacks. He logged three hundred hours of flying time, got a pilot's license, and trained in a Boeing 727 simulator. Federal investigators say it was Atta who was the operational commander and leader of the sleeper cell turned execution cell that meticulously carried out the attacks. The friends of this broken, depressed man now stared at the face of pure evil on television screens all over Cairo. The student who once got angry over the death of an insect was now responsible for the deaths of thousands. In a letter found in his luggage, a passage read, "Let each find his blade for the prey to be slaughtered."[2]

The little bird had sung.

Pimped Good

The story of Mohamed Atta, the pilot of the first airplane that brought hell to the north tower of the World Trade Center on September 11, is a profile of how your average guy can be moved to do the unspeakable when the right forces are in play. His issues are common to man and give us insight into how the war in the world around us is shaped by the invisible war for the souls inside us. He was no different from a fundamentalist "Christian" abortion-clinic bomber or a polygamist cult leader who abuses women and makes them his wives at age fourteen.

Atta is simply more memorably tied to a greater day of infamy in America's history than Pearl Harbor. He is the extreme side of the pendulum of evil. But before we divorce ourselves from such an evil man under the complete control of Satan and his MABs, we need to see that the common issues of manhood create the same opportunities for Satan's agents to focus on us.

- Lack of a strong identity: He had no sense of self.
- Lack of purpose: He was searching for significance.
- Lack of belonging: He was isolated relationally.
- Lack of influence: He was potentially more than what he had become.
- Lack of adventure: He was bored.
- Lack of transcendence: He was unconnected to the eternal.

Mohamed Atta was ripe for his conversion to Islamofascism. Give a man, or a people for that matter, a strong-enough identity and a purpose worth dying for, and that is when he'll start to believe anything. Yep, evil pimped Mohamed Atta pretty good.

But that's not any of us, right? Ask yourself a few questions: Is your identity strong enough for complete surrender? Are you undivided between what you believe and how you actually live and think? Are you meaningfully connected to other men, feeling shared convictions and a strong direction? Do you believe you are a man of influence with a chance to be great in some way? Are you bored with your life, wife, family, or career and feeling stuck? Are you making choices now that will outlive your life on earth? Are you investing your life into something that transcends yourself? Are you living your life with intention, direction, and motivation? Do you know where you are headed as a man?

All these questions speak to your vulnerability to outside control by the forces of evil. Satan and his assassins on assignment can coerce and deceive any of us into being their unwitting "perfect soldier." Without clear answers to questions of identity, purpose, and life investment, we are susceptible to suggestion, direction, and other foreign ideas that capable men like you have swallowed repeatedly throughout the ages.

"He was the perfect soldier: he went where you sent him, stayed where you put him, and had no idea of his own to keep him from doing exactly what you told him," wrote novelist Dashiell Hammett. I like the way rap artist Minister RMB articulates the same sentiment when he poetically calls out, "The devil's a pimp. Don't be his ho." Crass, authentic, and biblically accurate. The Devil and his demon recruiters prostitute good men and rob them of greatness. They do this by tapping into our broken manhood, frailties, insecurities, fears, and lack of total surrender to Jesus Christ.

How does God's man become less vulnerable to demonic influence and control? Easy. Drive a long blade through the heart of compromise and spiritual compartmentalization. Take away demonic footholds by surrendering to the Holy Spirit's leadership in *every area* of your life, no matter the cost. Of course, that's easier said than done and requires constant vigilance. But to go on the offensive we'll launch in section 3, we have to remember who we're really fighting. The Bible says it's not people, it's MABs—those murderous angelic beings.

chapter 9

devil winds

The LORD said to Satan, "The LORD rebuke you, Satan! The
LORD, who has chosen Jerusalem, rebuke you! Is not this man
a burning stick snatched from the fire?"

—ZECHARIAH 3:2

Fritz Coleman is the weatherman for the local NBC affiliate in Southern
California. He is so well known and trusted that a lot of locals defer
directly to him. "Well, Fritz said it was going to be sunny." "Fritz didn't
say it would be bad." This is a sign that you have become an icon: when
you become someone's first thought when it comes to any given topic.
Fritz *is* weather. Of course, the irony of all this is that he repeats the exact
same forecast for the majority of the year.

Ours is the least complicated weather pattern on the planet, and Fritz has,
in my opinion, an easier go of it than, say, a Seattle or Dallas guy. In fact,
there are only two situations that get him really jacked up: the occasional
rains and the Santa Ana wind conditions that hit us hard in the fall. The
rains require a little more energy from Fritz because, unfortunately, rain is

news in these parts—we covet it and loathe it at the same time. By default, we are also the world's worst drivers in the rain. Sport utility vehicles in these parts are for novelty, not a necessity. The winds, however, evoke a more serious demeanor from Fritz—an apprehensive one. You see, the Santa Ana winds in Southern California are synonymous with danger and devastation.

I came face to face with the dangers these winds pose on New Year's Eve 1994. We had friends over to bring in the new year, we finished cleaning up, and I hit the rack at about two o'clock in the morning. At three o'clock I heard my neighbor's big tree hitting the side of our house. It was obvious that this eerie, howling wind was giving that tree (and my house) a good spanking. First would come the wind and the simultaneous rustling of branches, and then *bonk!* There would be a lull for ten seconds, and then the next freight train would land on our house. I was mesmerized. But that changed when I noticed the windows in my bedroom inhaling and exhaling like a person with each blast of air. Still lying down, but very awake now, I wondered if the wind could actually implode my bedroom window. *Naw!* I thought. *Don't be silly.* Two seconds later, *WUH-BAM-CLANG!*

It was a surreal feeling bordering on denial. Imagine some guy standing outside my second-story bedroom window, reaching back, and throwing a huge brick through my window at my head. Howling winds were screaming at me now through a huge, jagged hole in the window, and my (now very terrified) wife was awake and screaming.

Impulsively I sat up, and that's when the blood started flowing down my face in several places. A large, jagged chunk of glass had been caught by the curtain and dropped on my forehead. Rising from the bed with glass crunching under my feet, I said, "I'm bleeding, honey. I'm going to the hospital. Go sleep in Cara's room."

That was my first up-close-and-personal encounter with Southern California's famous "devil winds." I also learned that where we lived (at the base of a canyon) produced a special phenomenon called "shearing Santa Ana wind conditions" or "double devil winds." The gust that blew out my window was double the normal velocity and hit the window at seventy to ninety miles per hour.

Impulsively I sat up, and that's when the blood started flowing down my face in several places.

The Santa Ana winds are considered dangerous because they knock things over (or out, in my case), but this danger pales in comparison to the fear of having these winds exploited by lightning-induced fires or, worse, an arsonist. In the last decade, you may have seen on CNN fantastic images of our beautiful coastlines, canyon communities, and regional forests glowing red from wildfires driven by these powerful winds. In fact, even as I type this sentence, Southern California is once again glowing red in fourteen different locations. The firefighters on the front lines are battling the devil winds and, as arson investigators have discovered, an arsonist who decided to exploit them with a well-placed spark.

Outside my back porch, one ridge over, is the glowing red aurora of the Santiago Canyon fire, threatening my home. This is the second time I have been through this since moving here in 1989. It is also the second time an arsonist was the culprit. This must be his magnum opus, because this is the perfect firestorm, as it is simply overwhelming my region of the state. The evacuations connected to these fires driven by devil winds in Southern California have reached the hundreds of thousands.

As I write, I am glued to the television, and lo and behold, there is my man Fritz leading off the top story of *NBC Nightly News* with Brian Williams talking about the Santa Ana wind conditions driving this fiery apocalypse. "Fritz Coleman may be the best-known weatherman in all of California," Williams opens. "He's a veteran of our NBC station in L.A." Fritz grabs the baton and is in his element. In essence, Fritz said, "What we have, Brian, is a large high-pressure system spinning clockwise over Nevada, Utah, and Colorado producing hot air and catapulting it toward the low-pressure system off the Southern California coast…"[1]

Brian Williams parlays Fritz's comments into an object lesson, calling my attention to satellite images recently taken high above Southern California showing the familiar coastline region bleeding humongous chains of white smoke from the affected wildfire areas. The view from space is spectacular—that's us burning down there.

These days I am an armchair meteorologist when it comes to the devil winds. I guess after getting smacked by them, I wanted to know. But my little ER visit and some stitches are nothing compared to the losses being suffered by families seeing their lives go up in arsonist-instigated smoke. It's like the arsonist was waiting for this, saw Fritz, picked his spots, and threw the flame. The bottom line: two pressure systems were exploited to create maximum destruction.

Whoever this coward was, he knew plenty of other factors would act like accelerant for the Santiago Canyon fire (the one in my backyard). This year we received only one-tenth our normal rainfall. There was also very low humidity, lots of dry brush and dead trees, and tough access to mountainous terrain. Having learned from the John Orr story how such cowards think, we know this perverted little man who set the sixteen-thousand-acre fire near me is somewhere getting off on this, watching everyone scramble, flee, and sob. He loves it. This symphony of destruction has been conducted just like he wanted.

When I watch the local news and hear Fritz say that he has "red flag wind advisories" in effect for south Orange County, I am *all* ears, but not because I am gun-shy. I am "flame shy," if that makes sense.

More concerned than me are the people who will be called on to flight the flames. Firefighters in Orange County are on high alert when intel on the weather pattern shows high pressure over states to the northeast of Southern California and low pressure off the coast. The strike teams are ready to deploy to hot-spot areas that flare up and threaten structures, homes, and lives. These teams are trained to establish a defensive line to save threatened homes. Air assault teams involving helicopters and fixed-wing aircraft are also on high alert when pressure conditions coalesce to produce the devil winds.

They follow the weather closely under normal conditions, and they follow it aggressively when the Santa Ana pattern forms. This kind of aggressive awareness, discernment, and preparation in response to the inevitable realities of our weather in Southern California serves as a living parable God's man can learn from in fighting evil.

Perfect Pressure Systems

Spiritually, God's man must see himself as under perpetual devil-wind conditions. He must train himself to see, read, and respond daily to this highly volatile and fluid spiritual environment. We must be ready to act preemptively in guarding ourselves against specific pressure systems at play that create dangerous conditions. And we must come to terms with the fact that there is a coward hiding in the darkness who will put matches to the fuel of momentum these pressures create.

The Bible lays out both the pressure systems and the players in detail. Our "Fritz" is the apostle Paul. Reporting live from the spiritual battlefield, he shares the details of the firestorms that ravage men's lives to this day, the forces that pull those storms into being, and unmasks the coward throwing matches into the mix:

> As for you, you were dead in your transgressions and sins, in which you used to live when you followed the *ways of this world* and of the *ruler of the kingdom of the air,* the spirit who is now at work in those who are disobedient. All of us also lived among them at one time, gratifying the *cravings of our sinful nature* and following its desires and thoughts. Like the rest, we were by nature objects of wrath. (Ephesians 2:1–3)

The High-Pressure System of the World

Like the devil winds of Southern California, there's a strong spiritual pressure system in the culture against God's man. When Paul uses the word *kosmos,* he means "a system or organized way to think, lacking in God's influence." This high-pressure system of thinking and living is satanically inspired to separate people from God by powerful philosophies (or "isms"): tribalism, culturalism, secular humanism, relativism, intellectualism, hedonism, narcissism, materialism. These are some of the most powerful manifestations of Satan's influence in the world. All these isms place pressure on men to conform to their objects of worship and place beliefs or practices over God. These ways of the world have their origins in men but are inspired by the hater of men.

What we must realize is that the world's systems of thinking and being are under Satan's direction. He is the dominant and controlling influence in these systems as prince of this world. We know this because as men give themselves to these isms, they are seduced farther from God and aren't able to reconcile their worldly

These ways of the world have their origins in men but are inspired by the hater of men.

identities with their faith. There is no such thing, for example, as Christ-centered hedonism, materialism, or narcissism. These worldly beliefs are directed by Satan, are subservient to him, and achieve his aims.

These world systems are packaged and sold by Satan as popular opinions and prevailing cultural norms around the globe. This is how Satan hides. It's not the Devil, it's an outlook on life, a belief, or a perspective on things that's accepted in culture by the majority. Those norms and opinions create high-pressure cultural systems that demand conformity and exclude behaviors and beliefs consistent with faith in Christ. They're also focused on keeping you centered on self and preventing you from turning to God. These systems of beliefs and the behaviors that go with them *oppose* knowing, following, and serving Jesus Christ because they are engineered to discourage and downplay faith in God.

Throughout the centuries men have tried to blend the beliefs of these systems with faith in Christ. It can't be done. Jesus told us, "As it is, you do not belong to the world" (John 15:19). That's an identity statement. A short time later, John would exhort God's men to follow suit: "Do not love the world or anything in the world" (1 John 2:15). A disciple gets this, and solid God's men have been passing it along ever since that first huddle with Jesus. God's man watches out for this system of high pressure, is aware of it, does not get caught up in it, and above all does not conform to it. Conforming would be the equivalent of getting swallowed by the high pressure—to stop being God pleasers and become man pleasers. Big or small cultural invitations that pressure God's man to think or behave in a way contradictory to faith in God are satanic. They amount to pressure from the outside seeking to make its way into our will, to control it and direct it.

This high-pressure system of culture is continuously spinning beliefs, behaviors, and identities specific to men. It is constant and powerful. More important, it is being directed *intentionally* toward the inviting low-pressure systems of our souls. Like a magnet to steel, the flow of evil energy is inevitable and inexorable. The high-pressure devil winds of the world are designed to flow toward one destination of low pressure.

The Low-Pressure System of the Flesh

The high-pressure system of cultural evil gains momentum by collaborating with the low-pressure system of man's sinful nature. Combining pressure systems creates devil winds in nature, and Satan uses the ways of the world to create a symbiotic, synergistic target in men's hearts. He's engineered the high-pressure system to seek out the low-pressure system of our flesh: our inherited predisposition to do evil. Even without Satan, this corrupted part of our character would go on sinning without encouragement.

He's designed the ways of the world to be attracted to this character flaw, and he needs the flesh for his systems' survival and success. Like a world-class symphony, Satan's score is designed as a dance of wills, a sonata of souls, to woo our spirits. The flesh is deeply attracted to the world at all levels—emotional, physical, material, and spiritual. Satan wants man to love the world, but the only way he can do this is through the flesh, enticing man to forsake his first love and commit spiritual adultery with the world and, by proxy, with Satan himself. Well acquainted with the cravings of our sinful nature, he makes it easy for the world to become the object of those appetites.

When the high-pressure system of the world and the low-pressure system of the flesh coalesce, you have the perfect situation for Satan to operate in. With the devil winds blowing fierce and hard, Satan times his flame, ignites a man's life, and creates a firestorm of evil designed to consume the believer, nullify his witness, and destroy his spiritual work.

Satan was kicked out of heaven, but he rules this world and its systems. It's his version of a pseudoheaven. In the world, he can receive the worship he coveted in heaven. Leader after leader lies in the ashes of his firestorms, overwhelmed by an unseen but active foe. Add to this the accelerating drought that combines with his high-pressure system to magnify his power, and we can see how God's man can unwittingly create the context for the perfect firestorm with

- a dry spirit—a life unwatered by the Word of God
- isolation—a life unwatered by authentic and honest connections to the body of Christ
- prayerlessness—a life unwatered by humility and faith and replaced with the dry tinder of self-sufficiency and pride
- negative emotions—a life unwatered by the love, peace, patience, and joy of the Holy Spirit
- secrets—a life unwatered by the freedom only honesty with God, self, and others can provide

The spiritually dry, emotionally depleted, relationally isolated, and morally vulnerable man *will be exploited.* Count on it. Satan will engineer the pressures within and without. Exerting his own pressure with flawless timing, he will then exploit all the variables and consume the man. He does this to have his heaven on earth, his own imitation trinity—the world, the flesh, and himself. "Satan works by imitation," notes E. M. Bounds. "It is his policy to make something as close to the original as possible and, thereby, break the force and value of the genuine."[2]

> *The spiritually dry, emotionally depleted, relationally isolated, and morally vulnerable man will be exploited.*

The Mimic

This unholy trinity is what makes our fight against evil so highly personal and significant. Satan's knock-off trinity needs *our complicity and cooperation with the flesh* to be complete. The simplest and most effective way to cut off the pseudotrinity is to listen to the Word instead of the world. Whenever there's a moral or relational issue in our lives, we must not listen to the world for direction and so allow the devil-wind conditions in our lives to feed our flesh, cut off God's power in our lives, and replace the operation of the true holy Trinity.

When God's man understands Satan's end game, he is less likely to become a pawn in it. Regardless of his spiritual condition, no man knowingly *likes* to be pimped like a common jerk for someone else's gratification and benefit. Satan, the wannabe God, tried to sell it to Jesus, but He didn't bite, and neither will His men. Satan is defeated, but he's in denial. He grasps at glory by getting man to exalt the world without reference to God. He accepts this pseudoworship because his character won't allow him to be worshiped for who he really is. Overt satanic worship just isn't attractive to the masses. He receives far greater vicarious worship through his servant, the world.

In this wannabe's version of the trinity, Satan assumes the role of creative mind, becoming like God. Man, through his flesh, becomes the incarnate expression of that mind in place of Jesus. And the world, with its system of godless philosophies, becomes the agent and active power, filling and empowering man from within in place of the Holy Spirit. God's plan for man is for redemption and relationship through the Son. Satan's plan is for revenge and retribution—to stick it to God and create separation from His sons—the old terrorist tactic of hurting a dad by taking his kids.

This is the context for truly discerning Satan's activities and all that we've been learning about in this chapter. When we see the *true motives* and discover them to be ignoble, selfish, and narcissistic, we realize something fundamental.

Now you know Satan at the deepest of levels. What do you think?

I am not a weatherman, but I want to be a Fritz in your life. I want you to understand the spiritual terrain, the landscapes, the amplifying factors, the insidious conductor of this requiem that tries to play us. As a fellow God's man and strike-team firefighter, I'm deployed to fight the flames of Satan's evil conflagration. I'm telling you to prepare for the pressures at play. Don't be exploited. Preempt the pressure of the world with a strong identity with, loyalty to, and duty in Christ. Preempt the flesh by honestly acknowledging your weaknesses, being open to help from God and people, and by rearranging your life so that sin no longer looks good.

You must do this because *you* (tap your chest again for me) are on the front lines of this wildfire condition on earth between eternities. While the flames are threatening and unpredictable, *you* must defend and save.

Your *own* discernment of the devil winds is critical. *You* must understand your own firestorm conditions, the high and low pressures, and the particular ways in which the Arsonist comes to exploit you. You must not make the conditions in your own life worse by being spiritually isolated and parched, unwatered by losing your healthy connections to God's Word and other God's men. Others are counting on you to be knowledgeable, strong, capable, trained, and present *for them*. We need to be clear: *Earth* is a firestorm of spiritual struggle, and you are in the middle of it. God has called us to fight this fire with all energy and wisdom. And with greater discernment comes greater confidence amid the flames.

Remember, your spiritual weatherman said it was going to be like this.

chapter 10

not an enigma: part one

Know ye that the ancient enemy doth strive by all means to
hinder thy desire to be good and to keep thee clear of all religious exercises.... Many evil thoughts does he suggest to thee
so that he may cause a weariness and horror in thee.

—THOMAS À KEMPIS

In April 1941 off the coast of Norway, an unsuspecting German trawler
was seized carrying precious cargo: two Enigma machines and the naval
Enigma settings for the previous month. These machines, which looked
like simple typewriters, contained the secret to encrypted Nazi communications previously impenetrable by the Allies. The technology was as
simple as it was complex, providing innumerable permutations of code.
German Enigma operators could type in a message, scramble it, and use
the receiver machine to unscramble it with the specific settings.

The Enigma code's Rosetta stone was the machine, and the key was its
monthly settings. It turned out to be the gift that kept on giving victories
for the Allies and ultimately led to significant defeats for the Nazis.

Once captured, Enigma was less of a puzzle and more of a road map to preempt the Nazis' war operations on sea, on land, and in the air. Shortly after, a few other seized machines and code books were captured from other German vessels and studied at Britain's now-famous code and cipher school at Bletchley Park. Scores of mathematicians and analysts were working out Enigma's settings with great success and passing along the information to Allied war planners. Among the bigger results:

- exposure of German military buildups prior to the invasion of Greece
- a coordinated Allied ambush allowing capture of German U-boats that had been paralyzing Allied shipping lanes in the North Atlantic
- interception of Gen. Erwin Rommel's communications to Rome and Berlin from North Africa
- intercepts allowing Allied code breakers to direct ships away from dangerous waters where German U-boats were hunting
- prevention of the loss of Egypt to German forces in 1942 which, war historians say, would have upset the timetable for the invasion of France

As British general Harold Alexander said, "The knowledge not only of the enemy's precise strength and disposition, but also how, when and where he intends to carry out his operations brought a new dimension to the prosecution of the war."[1]

The lesson? In war, predictability means success.

Predictable Patterns

The Bible assumes that God's man has broken Satan's code and knows his movements in advance. "For we," Paul writes, "are not unaware of his schemes" (2 Corinthians 2:11). Only fools who *want* to be defeated fail to learn what they're in for. Men will go to great lengths to predict the movements of the competition in business, politics, or sports. Think Patton reading Rommel's books on tank warfare. Think Patriots coach Bill Belichick filming signals of opposing teams' defensive coordinators. Think insider trading on Wall Street. Think CIA, Interpol, and Mossad—all of these endeavors simply to predict the opposition's next move.

God's men learn to discern Satan in three ways. First, we detect him by his core character traits. He leaves fingerprints. Seeing those characteristics manifested tips us off. By familiarizing ourselves with *who he is,* we can learn to smell the rat. This raises our spiritual perception by intuition and inference.

The second method is by understanding the instruments of evil that he uses to manipulate and destroy men from within and without. We learn about his networks of power, his connections and associations with cultures and men. He needs as his base of operations a world system in league with your dark impulses. We gain an upper hand on the underworld by learning how the world, the flesh, and the Devil together create a trifecta of trouble and a powerful axis of evil.

The third way we recognize Satan is by observation and study. This is warfare through hard intelligence and seeing repeated patterns. We study the film of his interactions with men. We dissect his angles of attack. We make mental notes of the strategies he favors and uses successfully. We raise our awareness and look for him to use those same ploys in various forms. This is what the Bible means when it says God's man is "not ignorant of [Satan's] schemes" (2 Corinthians 2:11, NASB). Literally, we know his playbook, and it's game on for us.

Cornerbacks in the National Football League call it "jumping a route" when they recognize a certain passing formation prior to the snap. They will trick the opposing quarterback into thinking they don't know what's coming, let him run the play, and then intercept the pass. Good basketball point guards do the same thing, as do savvy soccer players. When they steal the ball, these guys seem so fast that they must know the intentions of their opponents. At least 50 percent of that quickness is mental. These guys are thinking a step ahead, anticipating the opponents' moves in advance.

God's man is called to jump the route on the Enemy. It's all there in the playbook. Spiritually, it means we should expect his movements, discern them ahead of time, and move to preempt and confront them—or to prepare ourselves to take a hit for a higher purpose. He's coming, and he's creative. Satan's moves are prepared, well timed, organized, and thoughtful. He's not in a hurry. As we've learned, he waits for the right conditions. His timing is impeccable, and most of the time, he's a real gentleman at first.

So study these plays. They're the ones he runs over and over. Expect them all to happen in the realm of the mind.

Expect Mental Suggestion

Every thought that encourages you to violate the express will of God is from Satan. He understands the power of suggestion, and he knows he has a friend in you—your dark side that's begging for indulgence. Satan's suggestions are always intellectually, emotionally, sensually, or physically gratifying. His suggestions

> *Satan's suggestions are always intellectually, emotionally, sensually, or physically gratifying.*

always go to your need in the moment—for something new, comforting, reassuring, satisfying, or intriguing. Every suggestion is pregnant with pain, but that's never revealed.

Look at how he made a run at Eve:

> "Did God *really say*, 'You must not eat from any tree in the garden'?... You will not surely die," the serpent said to the woman. "For God knows that when you eat of it your eyes will be opened, and you will be like God, knowing good and evil." (Genesis 3:1, 4–5)

Translation: "God didn't tell you the full truth. If you stick to His way, you'll miss out. He's preventing your development and fulfillment. You should trust yourself on this one. Aren't you curious?"

God's man should audibly counter with, "Every word of God is flawless; he is a shield to those who take refuge in him. *Do not add to his words,* or he will rebuke you and prove you a liar" (Proverbs 30:5–6). God's man loves clear instruction, clear boundaries that protect him and amplify God's voice, and the joy of obedience. If God feels the need to speak His mind on something, no other opinion matters. Be ready to respond to the suggestion with the facts. Body-slam all suggestions by Satan with a simple, smash-mouth response.

fight fact
Satan elevates personal opinions over God's spoken Word. He always suggests a lack of fairness, equity, and benefit in God's way. He always implies you'll miss out if you don't act, which justifies your fleshly impulse in the moment and seems reasonable. Satan loves the gray areas, blurring the lines and muffling God's voice.

There are only two possible responses: *consideration* or *obliteration*. Eve used the first, and Jesus the second, audibly responding every time.

Satan says, "*If* you are the Son of God, *tell* this stone to become bread" (Luke 4:3). Jesus audibly counters with, "It is written: 'Man does not live on bread alone'" (verse 4). The God-Man gives the Suggester a piece of His mind on the subject—God's mind. This ends the discussion on this temptation and reaffirms His commitment to God. I don't know how long the pause was between the suggestion and the response. The Scripture simply says, "Jesus answered." Jesus smashed Satan's words and modeled an important principle for our fight against evil.

fight fact

For every suggestion that counters the Word of God, there's an answer from the Word of God.

The big question is: are there bullets in your magazine? Jesus pulls the trigger, and you hear, *Pow! Pow! Pow!* If you are not loading the magazine of your heart with sufficient ammo from the Scripture, the suggestion will come and all you will hear in response is, *Click! Click! Click!* Can you imagine a marine telling his gunnery sergeant, "Oops! Sorry, Sarge. Forgot to bring those pointy-shaped things." I feel stupid just saying it, much less doing it. That's not a soldier, that's a dead man.

No, a fighting God's man audibly counters all satanic suggestion with holy proclamation. "The mouth of the righteous man utters wisdom," the Psalmist reports. "The law of his God is in his heart; his feet do not slip" (Psalm 37:30–31). *Pow!* A confident, well-aimed squeeze on the holy trigger will suffice. God's man does not entertain satanic suggestion; he kills it with intent and purpose. He can't speak the Word of God and transgress it at the same time. Always greet the Sultan of Suggestion with a Word of welcome.

Expect Moral Temptation

Satan does not concern himself with you when you're eating cereal, brushing your teeth, or making a pit stop. These are physical functions that don't affect your relationships with God and people. However, the moment you cross into the world where your character can express itself in conduct, he's there. Satan crafts moral temptation to fit hand in glove with *you*. In his malicious and perverse way, he's looking to meet the specific needs of his "customer." He does his homework, pulls up your past, examines your insecurities, studies your tendencies, considers your vulnerabilities, researches your triggers, and investigates your less noble ways of dealing with pressure, stress, and responsibility. Satan never *accidentally* tempts a man. This means his timing always coalesces with what's going on *inside a man at any given moment. Get that.*

Watch the film, study the approach, and identify the objective:

Satan targets David: "One evening David got up from his bed and walked around on the roof of the palace. From the roof he saw a woman bathing. The woman was very beautiful, and David sent someone to find out about her" (2 Samuel 11:2–3). Satan's thinking, *Let's see. Male, visually stimulated, powerful, conqueror-type, successful, entitled, used to getting what he wants, pressure of a war. Not there. Needs to conquer something. Got it! Naked hottie taking a bath. Perfect.*

Check out his trap: "In the spring, *at the time when kings go off to war,* David sent Joab out with the king's men and the whole Israelite army.

They destroyed the Ammonites and besieged Rabbah. *But David remained in Jerusalem*" (2 Samuel 11:1). Bored insomniac not doing what he's supposed to do. "Take a little walk, David. Get some fresh air. Clear your head. Here. This should occupy your time for a while. Looky there!" Unlike with Eve, Satan didn't have to create doubt about God's goodness. David's isolation, emotional state of mind, and male hard-wiring were enough to create an ambush of the flesh.

Satan's goal? Hold out the promise of deep satisfaction outside the will of God and introduce a second will—David's. Exploit the moment, his kingly position, his entitlement, his gender weakness, his loneliness, his boredom, and his lack of purpose. *Boom*—a wedge is driven between David and God. Satan sets up the explosives to detonate with consequences that will continue from this moment over years of guilt, shame, and trouble.

> *Satan's goal? Hold out the promise of deep satisfaction outside the will of God and introduce a second will.*

Satan didn't waste this opportunity. He got his payoff from planning, timing, and flawless execution. Selective targeting is everything to Satan. Remember, he hit Jesus with the stone-to-bread suggestion only *after* Jesus was starving. The Scripture tells us specifically that Satan knows when a man is most vulnerable. "When the devil had finished all this tempting, he left him *until an opportune time*" (Luke 4:13).

Translation: Satan never wastes a temptation. He believes he will succeed because of his meticulous planning, timing, and tactics. His understanding of the nature of man and astronomical success rate don't hurt this confidence. "A man's disposition on the inside, i.e., what he possesses in his personality, determines what he is tempted by on the outside," notes

Oswald Chambers. "The temptation fits the nature of the one tempted, and reveals the possibilities of the nature. Every man has the setting of his own temptation, and the temptation will come along the line of the ruling disposition."[2]

Whatever is ruling your emotions at the time will be used against you when he strikes. In fact, you can predict with reasonable certainty when Satan will strike if you answer the following questions:

- Where am I when I am most tempted or vulnerable?
- Who am I with? or not with?
- How am I feeling? (Tired, lonely, bored, stressed, conflicted, angry, boxed in, discouraged, etc.)
- What time of day is it?
- Am I in conflict with anybody?
- What are my core insecurities, fears, or triggers?
- What situations cause me to get defensive?

Know the answers to these questions and take precautions, because Satan certainly knows the answers even if you don't! Know yourself, and determine when you are vulnerable, so you can guard against attack. If you don't think it can happen to you, remember: David was *the man.* Ask the many husbands, fathers, pastors, and Christian leaders in the body of Christ who know God and love Him but lost it all because they had a blind spot Satan was plotting to exploit. They never saw it coming. Satan does *his* homework even when *we* don't.

There's no escape from the testing ground of temptation. God said it would come—and in fact, it's necessary in order to develop a real man and bring him into greater service. It's no sin to be tempted. Jesus was tempted in every way. What is necessary is for God's men to expect it, preempt it, resist it, and not RSVP to the Tempter.

You *will* encounter temptation. The question is, whose man are you? Are you encountering the same types of temptation today as you did many years ago? The static or changing nature of the temptations you face reflects your growth in Christ and as a man.

Withholding submission of a certain area in your life ensures spiritual stagnation. As your character grows and changes, the attacks change too. Satan doesn't attack a babe in Christ the same way he does a mature, disciplined soldier. The tactics change based on your resolve and spiritual disposition. He only changes his tactics if he can't continue to hold you hostage through the impure passions he exploited before.

Nail this down: God's plan is not immunity from the struggle but victory over the temptation. God told the men of Israel that He would give them the land and that they would be victorious. A lot of men hearing this promise were elated. But they went from elation to deflation when they realized they'd need to suit up, show up, and engage the people hand to hand to receive it. They wanted God to simply hand it over. But what good would that do? Would they have appreciated it as much in the long run? And would giving it to them outright have produced the faith their Commander was really looking for?

You are already victorious over Satan in Christ. Not only has God said it, Christ has accomplished it. The second part is harder to swallow—and requires faith. That is, while you and I are victorious, we can't escape the battle just yet. We must head into the fight with that promise from Christ strapped under our belts—He has given us power over our enemy, and He will help us achieve the victory. Guys who get this are commended in the Scriptures as having a different spirit.

We need fighters who discern evil, who walk in victory over the Enemy, who are willing to show up every time. I realize that only a few will have this kind of spirit, but I'm praying that you will be one of them. Dare to submit to God's promise not just in your comfort but in a willingness *to fight*.

Roll the film on how Caleb responded to the promise by running to battle.

> At the end of forty days they returned from exploring the land....
>
> They gave Moses this account: "We went into the land to which you sent us, and it does flow with milk and honey! Here is its fruit. But the people who live there are powerful, and the cities are fortified and very large...."
>
> Then Caleb silenced the people before Moses and said, "We should go up and take possession of the land, for we can certainly do it."
>
> But the men who had gone up with him said, "We can't attack those people; they are stronger than we are...."
>
> Joshua son of Nun and Caleb son of Jephunneh, who were among those who had explored the land, tore their clothes and said to the entire Israelite assembly, "The land we passed through and explored is exceedingly good. If the LORD is pleased with us, he will lead us into that land, a land flowing with milk and honey, and will give it to us. Only do not rebel against the LORD. And do not be afraid of the people of the land, because we will swallow them up.

Their protection is gone, but the LORD is with us. Do not be afraid of them." (Numbers 13:25, 27–28, 30–31; 14:6–9)

It's fine to believe in Christ's victory over Satan at the cross. We all need to believe in that promise of Satan's ultimate defeat. But it's a far different thing to step out on that promise and fight when you're outsized, outmanned, outsmarted, and outmatched in every way. Jesus has told His guys they've already won, but how many are ready to walk in that promise and actually fight? "I have given you authority to trample on snakes and scorpions and *to overcome all the power of the enemy; nothing will harm you.* However, do not rejoice that the spirits submit to you, but rejoice that your names are written in heaven" (Luke 10:19–20). In other words, "You have already won by virtue of your salvation, and it's not of you, but of *Me*. Don't get played by Satan and attach to the power. Simply walk in My promise. Have faith!"

Caleb chose not to focus on the enemy but on the promise of God. A fighting God's man is not cowed by the Devil; he's caught up in the victory he knows God's already won. *That* sort of man is an unstoppable force, the kind of motivated fighter God is looking for. Listen to what God says about Caleb: "Because my servant Caleb *has a different spirit and follows me wholeheartedly,* I will bring him into the land he went to, and his descendants will inherit it" (Numbers 14:24). Which spirit did Caleb have? A willingness to fight and experience the promised victory *through the struggle.* He rejected the easy way the Devil always offers and stood for God's work, in him and through him.

Satanic suggestions should be expected to come at us every day, from all sides, and with great intensity. We are *in the land,* and we're to fight with the assurance of God's direction. If we can sacrifice our fear on the altar,

Satan's schemes will not be an enigma. Remember his file and God's promise of triumph.

We're almost ready to hit the ground. But there are still three more levels of satanic strategy to crack open, so stick with me.

Onward...

not an enigma: part two

Those who serve God are the ones who demand Satan's attention, provoke his anger, and call forth his strategies.

—E. M. BOUNDS

Ever thought about the term *passive-aggressive*? It's a complete oxymoron, but it actually describes a relational approach where a person may be smiling outwardly, shaking your hand, making promises, even compli- menting you, while at the same time he's obstructing your progress, steal- ing from you, sabotaging you, and possibly plotting your destruction.

Think of the vengeance-driven sociopath currying favor with someone who has hurt him in the past and with whom he is now playing chummy to get close so he can hurt the person back. Think of the pimp who lures the fifteen-year-old runaway into his web by playing the father figure, offering protection from and provision in a hard and hostile world, only to gain control of her to use her as a human slave. These are the obvious expressions, but the mentality can also be subtle: *do whatever it takes to create a bond in order to gain control and destroy.*

The passive-aggressive may send mixed messages or make big promises to help but then delays on the delivery, often never intending to make good on those promises. He makes life miserable for someone while setting a trap by ensuring the person still needs him. We call it *sleeping with the enemy*. And at some point, when the object of this twisted aggression realizes what's up and the aggressor recognizes that knowledge, the game devolves from cordial to openly hostile.

That's the progression that happens with Satan's strategy. Suggestion and temptation are his friendly ploys that make up his passive-aggressive mission in our lives. He acts like a best friend to soothe and stroke our sinful flesh, to offer ideas and solutions that play to our dark impulses, and to give us a crack-hit of pleasure. After he pimps us, he goes from friendly pimp to accuser, serving generous portions of guilt and shame to continue the cycle. "Boy, look what you're turning into. You must feel horrible. Here, try this."

This is about as friendly as Satan gets. Suggestion and temptation have a short but brief upside that ends abruptly with *you* holding the bag and suffering the consequences. Once you bite, Satan's out, his mission accomplished. Your flesh and the world take over after that. Plenty of God's men think they can play the Devil at his own game, but they end up hooked into the consequences phase with demons manipulating their emotions to keep them safely trapped.

Suggestion and temptation are Satan's best-selling lines, and they've been producing fantastic results for thousands of years.

But there's more. This progressive cycle predictably continues toward open hostility.

138

It's predictable because all he has are these same devices to use individually or in combination. But don't be tempted to believe this makes him easy to figure out. Even if you do get it, you still have to do something with the info. And that's what the third section of this book—on confronting him—is for. Once we're conscious of and familiar with his craft so that he's no longer an enigma, we'll focus on the counterattack. But for now, here are the final pieces on how to *anticipate* him.

Expect Mental Rationalization

Any time you're coming up with good reasons to do evil things (especially religious-sounding ones), look over your shoulder. Rationalization is Satan's most productive way of encouraging self-deception. This evil-inspired logic provides safe cover for Satan to hide himself in your thinking. With his encouragement, a little lawyer in your head will come out to strongly defend an attitude or action that's inconsistent with your faith, the Bible, and Christ's example. The voice offers intellectual, rational, logical, and passionate justifications for immoral behavior.

And worse, the little lawyer sounds like you. In fact, he *is* you, but he's being encouraged by Satan with plenty of logical ammo. We don't have to wonder why men become so smart and so dumb at the same time. We can all justify our wrong behavior and grow stupid enough to believe our own logic. Satan figures if we're dumb enough to hang ourselves by the noose of self-deception, the least he can do is provide the rope of rationalization.

> *He knows the exact logic that fits the agenda of the flesh and creates in the moment a rebuttal against the conscience.*

Satan's high intelligence makes him a sophisticated engineer of deception. He's an *artist* of the lie, both devious and deliberate. He knows the exact logic that fits the agenda of the flesh and creates in the moment a rebuttal against the conscience.

Think Ananias and Sapphira ("A & S"). They see people getting a lot of attention for doing charitable works in the early church, and they want to get in on the act. During this great birthing of the church, God was inspiring believers to do radical things like sell houses and distribute the money to people in need. It was quite an outpouring of generosity. A & S are watching all this go down, and suddenly they're inspired to pimp the situation for some recognition *and* some profit. Let's study the film of the "also-sold" couple.

> Now a man named Ananias, together with his wife Sapphira, also sold a piece of property. With his wife's full knowledge he kept back part of the money for himself, but brought the rest and put it at the apostles' feet.
>
> Then Peter said, "Ananias, how is it that Satan has so filled your heart that you have lied to the Holy Spirit and have kept for yourself some of the money you received for the land? Didn't it belong to you before it was sold? And after it was sold, wasn't the money at your disposal? What made you think of doing such a thing? You have not lied to men but to God." (Acts 5:1–4)

Poetic, isn't it? "Also sold" pretty much tells the whole story. A & S were sold an evil logic that they in turn sold to themselves and then proceeded to try to sell to God. Of course He couldn't buy it. Clearly the Evil One exploited what was already inside these two, using perverted logic to damage the early church's power and ministry in Jerusalem. And Peter nails them by putting the *thinking and logic* on trial to expose Satan. He spots rational lies being swallowed. Something tipped him off, and he knew Satan loves to exploit human logic and reasoning because it helps him achieve his main goal: *to introduce a second will, one other than God's.*

Evil rationalization takes us down the road from good to great. Good reasons, good validations, and good excuses are the perfect ingredients for the Great Liar to perform his artistic evil in your life. We must see *ourselves* in Ananias and Sapphira. We are made of the same stuff: emotions, insecurities, needs, wants, fears, and pride that evil logic and deception can exploit to drive a wedge between (1) you and God, (2) you and people, and (3) you and your purpose.

Combating satanic deception and rationalization always starts with the willingness to have a truth encounter with God, yourself, and others. When we refuse truth, we leave the door wide open to deception and destruction. Satan will custom-design deception to your inner disposition and relationship with the truth. Remember, he's in any dark part of your character that has yet to yield to the truth.

The solution? Kill your pride and love truth till it hurts. Prefer authenticity. Choose openness. Favor admitting over defending. Support the authority of Scripture in your life and discipline yourself to stop engaging in fantasy. Accept people and things *as they are* over how you wish they were. Deal with the hard things and don't deny their presence. Embrace the veracity of the Holy Spirit and question the goodness of your flesh. Let the facts speak and trust God with the solution. Reject and rebuke good reasons to do selfish and evil things. These are fighting behaviors of God's man.

Expect Accusation from Within

A prosecuting attorney asks the witness, "Do you see the person responsible for the crime in this room?" And in slow motion, the witness points to the defendant and says, "That's him right over there."

The attorney then says, "Let the record reflect that the witness has identified Mr. Outta Luck as present at the scene of the crime." Getting that witness to *point the finger* may not be conclusive, but it's *very persuasive.* It plants an image in the jury's mind that they won't be able to easily dismiss during deliberations. Every chance a prosecuting attorney gets to weaken or discredit the character of the defendant, the better his case gets.

For Satan, taking potshots at the character of God's man is an art form. Hitting below the belt? Definitely. Whatever it takes to undermine his reputation before God and man. Let's study the film of Satan's accusations in Job.

- God's opening statement: "Have you considered my servant Job? There is no one on earth like him; he is blameless and upright, a man who fears God and shuns evil."
- Accuser's rebuttal: "Does Job fear God for nothing?... Have you not put a hedge around him and his household and everything he has? You have blessed the work of his hands, so that his flocks and herds are spread throughout the land. But stretch out your hand and strike everything he has, and he will surely curse you to your face" (Job 1:8–11).

In the spiritual world, Satan is one of those creatures who loves going to small-claims court to nitpick. The Bible has crowned him the King of Sour Grapes, the one who is "the accuser of our brothers, who accuses them before our God day and night" (Revelation 12:10). Don't miss this: relent-lessly pointing the finger at God's people is Satan's job description. Emo-tionally, he is like a category-five tornado swirling with anger, making large sucking sounds, yanking people up by the roots, displacing them without mercy, tossing them around, and dumping them in some distant emo-tional cornfield. *That's* what the Devil purposes to do every day to God's people whenever and wherever the opportunities present themselves.

God allows him to make these arguments but dismisses them because of the believer's representation in Christ. We have an "Advocate with the Father" (1 John 2:1, NASB) who provides us with complete immunity against any charge. When Satan presents in the court of divine opinion, nothing sticks. *However,* when Satan puts man on trial in front of man, it's a different story. A lot of us have a past, some of us have regrets, and *everybody* owns hidden self-doubts, insecurities, frailties, wounds, defects, and fears. These accessories of the fallen nature act like an adhesive for the Accuser to pin accusations on our spirits and discourage us. When a man gets a healthy dose of self-pity, self-despair, or self-condemnation, Satan arrives to *magnify* those thoughts and views to feel fatal and final. He loves to exaggerate the normal and elevate it to extremes. Like this:

- "I made a mistake" becomes "I *always* blow it."
- "I need to work on that" becomes "I'll *never* change."
- "Well, that didn't go well" becomes "Well, what did I expect?"
- "I may need some support in this" becomes "I could never talk about *that.*"
- "This is making me feel overwhelmed at the moment" becomes "Life is falling apart."
- "This isn't easy" becomes "How does this always happen to me?"
- "I need to figure this out" becomes "This is just like God to do this to me."

Misery loves company, and Satan is happy to oblige. He magnifies misery to obscure God, isolate you, and get you to medicate your despair with substitute pleasures. He says, "Get angry, get high, get nasty, get drunk, get on the Net, get even, just get busy." And the feeling changes for a while. But the end game is the same: a wedge is driven into your relationships—especially with other Christians, the people who are supposed to be there for help and healing. To keep you from turning outward toward help, Satan works hard to *keep you inside your own head.*

> *He magnifies misery to obscure God, isolate you, and get you to medicate your despair with substitute pleasures.*

In the end, remember this: whenever emotions, words, and conclusions begin to be exaggerated, take a deep breath, take a break, and take inventory of reality. Take *what's inside* to the God-approved sources *outside* for help.

Tell God what's going on inside and how you feel. Watch film of Jesus to learn how to do this. Watch Him battle it out:

> Then Jesus went with his disciples to a place called Gethsemane, and he said to them, "Sit here while I go over there and pray." He took Peter and the two sons of Zebedee along with him, and he began to be sorrowful and troubled. Then he said to them, "My soul is overwhelmed with sorrow to the point of death. Stay here and keep watch with me."
>
> Going a little farther, he fell with his face to the ground and prayed, "My Father, if it is possible, may this cup be taken from me. Yet not as I will, but as you will." (Matthew 26:36–39)

See what He does? He tells His best earthly buddies exactly what's going on *inside* His mind and heart. He is battling to do God's will, doing it with a ton of honesty, and not giving Satan a chance to mess with His emotions. He took them to God and to His friends. Although the disciples could not fix how Jesus felt, He just needed to interrupt the turmoil inside, dump it, and fight through it to do the right thing.

Are you in turmoil today? Go to God. Talk to Him. Then find a promise in the Scripture you can stand on (Romans 8:28 is great start) and surrender your will in the situation to God's. Follow this up by turning to a safe friend (spouse, if you're married) who will listen and who loves the Lord. Many times all you need to do is talk it out to see things aren't as bad as you felt. Receive the comfort of God's promise to redeem the situation and listen to what your friends have to say. *If you don't deal with how you feel inside, Satan will use what you leave to manipulate, exaggerate, and motivate you to find "solutions" that will harm you.* Satan does not like to be interrupted when he's streaming discouraging thoughts our way. These disciplines do just that and shut him down.

Expect Accusations from Christians

"Et tu, Brute!" fits the shock and awe of an attack coming from within your own circle. As his longtime-ally-turned-bad drove the knife in, Caesar cried, "You, Brutus!" If Satan can't get you to point the finger yourself, there are plenty of other unwitting fingers available to him. The evil reality of Christians accusing and abusing other Christians is a testimony to the craftiness and tactical genius of our ancient accuser.

To annihilate the church, attack God's glory, and strike a blow to Jesus, he can kill three birds with one stone by sowing division within God's people. As their common fears and pride permit, if he can get them fighting among themselves, discontent with and selfish toward their leaders and other Christians, they become his agents. Study the film: "You, my brothers, were called to be free. But do not use your freedom to indulge the sinful nature; rather, serve one another in love. The entire law is summed up in a single command: 'Love your neighbor as yourself.' If you keep on biting and devouring each other, watch out or you will be destroyed by each other" (Galatians 5:13–15).

The issue here is believer on believer. The Holy Spirit has been replaced by another spirit called *religion*. Someone's man-made standard has been breached, and the Holy Spirit has been fired. There are new deputies who've been appointed and are practicing character assassination in the name of God. A sure sign Satan has hijacked the church is a self-righteous and critical Christian taking on other Christians.

Martin Luther King Jr. was right: "We must learn to live together as brothers or perish together as fools." The Bible says that God's man counters accusation and division by keeping his eye on the ball: serve people in love, attach less to what people say and more to what God says, and let God deal with critics. Practically, if accusation is directed by someone we know well, Matthew 18 tells us how to manage it before it gets out of hand: "If your brother sins against you, go and show him his fault, just between the two of you.... But if he will not listen, take one or two others along.... If he refuses to listen to them, tell it to the church; and if he refuses to listen even to the church, treat him as you would a pagan or a tax collector" (verses 15–17). The high and narrow road is our path. "It's not the critic who counts," Teddy Roosevelt said. "The credit belongs to the man who is actually in the arena."

A fighting God's man concerns himself with the mission, not the mouths.

Expect Persecution

When the Devil fails to tempt, deceive, or discourage you through accusation, the only avenue left is the physical. I recently read an article about what happens when previously controllable people decide that "dealing with the devil" is not in their best interest: "Ten young women involved in prostitution have been murdered in Calgary. One of these was a 15 year-old girl. The man convicted of her murder wore a T-shirt that read: *Three can keep a secret when two are dead*."[1] The Great Pimp gets mad when his "prostitute" says to him, "I'm done with you." The gloves come off, the frustration comes out, and so do the fangs.

Jesus told us that for many of God's best men, it would come to this: "Blessed are those who are persecuted *because of righteousness,* for theirs is the kingdom of heaven" (Matthew 5:10). That persecution comes from Satan against a certain quality of man. Did you catch the italics? The more righteous you become, the higher the hostility factor. We are instructed to expect it because our commitment to God in this world calls for it.

Study the film, God's man:

> Dear friends, do not be surprised at the painful trial you are suffering, as though something strange were happening to you. But rejoice that you participate in the sufferings of Christ, so that you may be overjoyed when his glory is revealed. If you are insulted because of the name of Christ, you are blessed, for the Spirit of glory and of God rests on you. If you suffer, it should not be as a murderer or thief or any other kind of criminal, or even as a meddler. However, if you suffer as a Christian, do not be ashamed, but praise God that you bear that name. (1 Peter 4:12–16)

Open hostility in enemy territory is not unusual, it's to be expected. The world systems under Satan's control drive their respective cultures or governments to openly persecute Christians. Persecution comes to those on whom the Spirit and glory of God rest. Pseudo-Christians don't require persecution because they're already blending in nicely with the culture around them. The very life of God's man proves his allegiance as he lives within his particular culture and world system. It's a zero-sum tactic on Satan's part because persecution, while the most openly hostile tactic, is also the most counterproductive for Satan for a lot of reasons. If believers don't cave in, God is glorified. If believers suffer for their faith, they're made stronger.

Study the waves of persecution in the first and second century. The church exploded. Or look at modern-day communist China. Where up until recently it was illegal to even own a Bible under threat of imprisonment or death, according to Open Doors International there are presently more evangelical Christians in China than there are in the United States. My own encounters with the persecuted Tzotzil Indians of southern Mexico bear out the same principle—they've already won. When believers are openly persecuted, faith grows.

God's man is called to suffer with his Lord. Prepare for it, expect it in some form, thank God for it, and face it focused on eternity. Pray for God to use it for His purposes. We are not promised escape from it but deliverance in it. Suffering for the sake of Christ brings about a revelation of Christ to those who see it. In the end, persecution gets stuffed back in Satan's face. "We who are alive are always being given over to death for Jesus' sake, *so that his life may be revealed in our mortal body*" (2 Corinthians 4:11).

Satan has the world's cultural, political, and religious systems under his power, and he will use them to exact his vengeance against God through persecution of His people. If you're catching flak, know that it's because you're a son being molded into the image of the Son.

So that's all Satan's got: suggestion, temptation, rationalization, deception, accusation, and persecution. He runs the same plays over and over and over to introduce *a second will other than God's*—yours or his. That's why we must fight his schemes proactively and preemptively: "Your kingdom come, *your will be done*" (Matthew 6:10). Our proud tradition goes before us as God's men, and Satan's playbook is ours to use against him. Ignorance is not an option. Willingness must now take its place.

(For more information on the persecuted church and how you can help, go to the Open Doors Web site at www.odusa.org.)

hijacked

If, prior to the betrayal of our Lord, the disciples had discussed how they could most completely misunderstand the events surrounding Jesus' arrest, trial, and crucifixion, they could not have done a better job. What they perceived and what happened were exact opposites.

—WALTER HENRICHSEN

It was Christmas Eve. Excitement was in the air as the plane prepared for takeoff from Algiers headed for Paris. Everyone was going home for the holidays. Bags were being stowed, people were settling into their seats, and four security agents were checking passports throughout the cabin.

Suddenly, the cheerful Noel became a tearful hell. The hijacking of Air France Flight 8969 began with an intimidating shout: *"Allah is great!"* The doors were locked. The plane, its flight plan, crew, and passengers were taken hostage by the four men posing as Algerian security agents. In a split second, their future was lost.

The details, as reported a few weeks later by *Time* journalist Thomas Sancton, tell a chilling story of detailed planning, paralyzing fear, terrorist agendas, and incredible courage.

- The four terrorist–security agents planned the takeover to gain the release of imprisoned fellow terrorists.
- They would fly the plane to France and explode it over Paris.
- Three passengers were executed and thrown onto the tarmac in Algiers before the plane was given permission to fly to France.

The plane reached Marseilles, France, under cover of darkness at 3:30 a.m. on Christmas Day. The terrorists demanded twenty-seven tons of fuel be loaded onto the Airbus and set a literal drop-dead time line for departure, after which point passengers would be murdered for government noncompliance.

Trained French commandos, disguised as service personnel, were given permission to board the plane and deliver food and supplies. In the course of their "duties" the commandos gathered intelligence, planted listening devices, and ensured that the side doors of the plane were unlocked before being ordered to deplane.

As the plane was taxiing, the French commandos approached the plane on three mobile loading ramps, entered the plane from the front and rear doors, and proceeded to effect one of the most successful antiterrorist operations in history.

All four terrorists were killed, all one hundred seventy-three passengers and crew were freed, and twenty-five people were treated for wounds, only one serious.

Demolition experts confirmed that twenty sticks of dynamite had been strategically placed and set to be detonated inside the plane.[1]

Joy on earth (versus hell) returned for the crew and passengers that Christmas.

Such an attempt to throw it off along the way, no one could have predicted.

Loaded with Fuel

As we've seen, the spiritual world is rife with well-engineered and malicious plots designed to gain control of men, introduce a second agenda, and produce maximum devastation. As a consequence, the game that is "on" is a game of disciplined discernment of those plots. God's man is commissioned to be about the business of predicting and preempting the Terrorist's agenda much the same way a counterterrorism agent is deployed. We are appointed to know the schemes of the Devil, called to study them, trained to discern them, and prepared to come against them. Being outwitted is not a part of our tradition as a fighting group.

The easy part is identifying the tactics. The hard part is knowing when and where they will be used. In many instances you can't predict the situation. You simply have to be ready to respond.

This is the one advantage all terrorism has on the world of free men—the element of surprise. The Algerian terrorists' plans included taking over an existing flight to accomplish their mission. The situation was already loaded with leverage they didn't have to create. Twenty-seven tons of jet fuel? Check. Transportation to Paris? Check. Hostages? Check. All that was left was to figure out how to insert themselves undetected to take advantage of the situation and execute their mission.

Their *behavior* was predictable. But their methodology was creative.

To fight the dynamic of evil, we have to think like the terrorists and ask:

- What platforms exist that are available, volatile, and easy to exploit?
- What situations in our lives could be "loaded with fuel" for Satan and his emissaries?
- How might they surprise us, gain control, and take over the direction of our lives?
- How could evil hijack us and turn us into "flying bombs"?
- Where, when, and how might we be hijacked?

Think of your life as a busy airport. Then imagine that the numerous planes arriving and departing are the daily events of your life, involving relationships, potential circumstances, and many connections. Each day, these planes (or "relationship events") reach your airport and are serviced and reloaded with fuel. The fuel is your emotions giving life and meaning to each relationship and event, big and small. Every relationship event has gotten your personal clearance to land at your hub, and you're filling them up and putting them back in the air.

They're familiar flights with familiar faces. The bigger Airbuses include your spiritual journey, marriage, family, career, and future with massive amounts of emotional fuel. These relationship events have to fly long distances, carry tons of hopes and dreams, and deliver much happiness and meaning on arrival.

So *now,* think like a terrorist. Hijack just one of those Airbuses, and you've got a serious hostage crisis. And unlike Air France 8969, most hijackings do not have a happy ending.

How would a terrorist do it? First, he'd know that those planes can't go long without loading up on fuel. And second, he'd know that that fuel is the payload, the catalyst for potential destruction, so if he wants a big mess, he'll need a lot of it.

Know this: the Great Terrorist is aware that emotions fuel how we see and experience our reality, and those perceptions ultimately drive our behaviors.

We all know men whose perceptions were obscured by out-of-control emotions, and it led to a fireball falling from the sky. Rightly managed, emotions have the potential to get us to our destinations as God's men. But in the wrong hands, they can turn us into flying bombs. And yes, *Satan is very aware of this situation.*

> *Know this: the Great Terrorist is aware that emotions fuel how we see and experience our reality, and those perceptions ultimately drive our behaviors.*

Every man is like a hub for many Airbus 300s, loaded down with tons of fuel and each with devastating potential. An emotionally uncontrolled man is ripe for a hijacking. It's only by managing our emotions God's way that we can strike a blow to Satan and foil his plots.

Otherwise, we become a hijacking waiting to happen.

Crouching at the Door

The Bible not only tells us that emotions fuel our lives, it tells us that Satan is plotting to exploit them for his purposes if we don't manage them the right way. Satan knows that men are vulnerable and frustrated over their inability to control the people and events that impact their lives. More specifically, he knows that our inability to control events can precipitate a greater inability to keep control of our emotions.

Sadly, without intentional security measures, we're all easy to hijack. Study the film.

A Lack of Emotional Control Makes Us Vulnerable

"Like a city that is broken into and without walls is a man who has no control over his spirit" (Proverbs 25:28, NASB). An ancient city without walls was pretty much indefensible. In the same way, your life is either protected or made vulnerable by a wall of self-control over your reactions to relational events in your life. The man with "no control over his spirit" gets hijacked.

Unconfessed Resentment Gives Satan Power in Your Life

" 'In your anger do not sin': Do not let the sun go down while you are still angry, and do not give the devil a foothold" (Ephesians 4:26–27). See the picture? There's an elephant in the room, and it gets larger by the hour when it's not acknowledged, dealt with, and eliminated from human relationships. Unresolved anger in any form puts a neon Welcome sign up for evil.

> *Any form of anger not dealt with openly, honestly, and productively is, by default, given to Satan to use as a base of operation.*

Like me, you might be tempted to say, "I don't have a problem with anger." Fair enough. The problem, however, is that anger is simply the baseline emotion behind the *expressions* of it:

irritation	aggravation	agitation	annoyance
exasperation	frustration	rage	hostility
bitterness	resentment	scorn	vengefulness
contempt	envy	jealousy	coveting

Any form of anger not dealt with openly, honestly, and productively is, by default, given to Satan to use as a base of operation. We are given the freedom to be angry, but we are charged to be angered about the things God is angered about and to deal with the emotion responsibly. Anger is inevitable, but destruction is optional. Angry men make useless soldiers in the fight against evil. They've already been hijacked.

Out-of-Control Emotions Blind You to Satan's Presence

"Humble yourselves, therefore, under God's mighty hand, that he may lift you up in due time. *Cast all your anxiety on him because he cares for you.* Be self-controlled and alert. Your enemy *the devil prowls* around like a roaring lion *looking for someone to devour"* (1 Peter 5:6–8). Peter is talking to a group of people going through an emotionally turbulent time, and he does not want them to get hijacked in the midst of their suffering.

The encouragements are straightforward and effective: "Put yourself under God's authority, relieve the pressures inside by talking to God, and raise your threat level to Red." Why? Because if you don't, you become slow-moving prey. Instead, take away the Enemy's leverage.

Like anger, anxiety has a bunch of cousins, so if you're tempted to say, "I don't struggle with anxiety," think about how worry and fear manifest themselves in various behaviors:

overeating	workaholism	isolation
stress	edginess	apprehension
overcontrol	overplanning	avoidance

In fact, any negative emotional state we don't cast on God leads to anxiety. Sadness, suffering, disappointment, loneliness, lust, shame, pride, longing, hopelessness—all must be expressed to God instead of suppressed and made available to Satan. We pray certain psalms for this very reason. They express emotions to God, and as we express them to Him, our feelings begin to change. "I *sought the LORD, and he answered me*," David reflects, "he *delivered me from all my fears.* Those who look to him *are radiant;* their faces are never covered with shame" (Psalm 34:4–5).

A Christian is never told to cover up a real emotion. That plays right into Satan's hands. On the contrary, we're supposed to live in truth and reality and to experience emotions the way God created us to. Think Moses expressing his insecurities to God before accepting his mission to meet with Pharaoh. Think David in Psalm 51 after committing adultery. Think Jeremiah blaming God for his depression in Lamentations and then remembering God and finding joy again. Think Jesus in the Garden of Gethsemane. Paul told the Corinthians to mourn and weep with those who are mourning and weeping. In a world filled with trials and suffering, we must have a place to bring our struggles and inner conflicts.

God's man casts his emotions on a caring God; he does not conceal them. To hide what's really going on inside is *ungodly* and gives increasing control to Satan. God's man has a place to go with his struggles—to his

Maker and to his spiritual family. It is not one or the other, it is both at the same time. Both are commanded. One source provides spiritual healing and hope, the other provides emotional healing and support.

We must master our emotions the right way, or we will give in to the wrong way.

Study the film of Cain and Abel in Genesis. Two guys working hard who decide to worship God by giving Him an offering. One brother's attitude and motivation are off; the other's are right on. One was thoughtless; the other offered generous worship. God saw their hearts and responded appropriately as any father would if a child was insincere in his appreciation. "The LORD looked with favor on Abel and his offering, but on Cain and his offering he did not look with favor. So *Cain was very angry, and his face was downcast.* Then the LORD said to Cain, 'Why are you angry? Why is your face downcast? If you *do what is right,* will you not *be accepted*? But if you do not do what is right, sin is crouching at your door; it desires to have you, but you must master it" (Genesis 4:4–7).

God sees the perceptions Cain's emotions are creating. They are totally off. God speaks to him about it: "Don't believe your emotions. Believe Me! You're jealous and angry. Put away your pride and talk to Me. They're just emotions! I won't reject you no matter how mad you feel. Don't go to that place within, or evil will win. *Fight,* son!"

The picture communicated by the Hebrew word for "crouching" is that of an evil demon crouching at the entrance of a building. Here, again, is the picture of evil forces preying on a man who's emotionally unstable. His emotions have mastered him instead of the other way around. And he's stepped out from under God's loving authority and acceptance. He's given himself over to perceptions created by his emotions as if those perceptions were real. He believes God won't take him back and that his brother deserves to die. He takes the bait, and Satan wins. Cain gets hijacked and attacks his brother, Abel, and kills him.

God's message to God's man is the same: *master it.*

Pull the Handle

On a McDonnell Douglas Super 80 passenger jet, the biggest indicator lights on the instrument panel in front of the pilot are two large luminescent handles. These are the engine fire lights. The reason they are both handles and lights is to simplify the process of putting out a fire seven miles up. If one of the engines catches fire, the pilot starts a sequence of events with those handles to arrest a fire in an engine.

My buddy Paul (an MD-80 pilot) walked me through the sequence:

- The fire handle lights up, visually signaling to the pilot there's a fire.
- An audio signal or voice message tells him which engine is on fire.
- When the pilot pulls the handle, it shuts off fuel, oil, and hydraulics to that engine, and the fire retardant bottle is armed.
- The pilot rotates the lighted handle to release the retardant and put out the fire.

Negative emotions are like the instrument panel on that plane. They let God's man know something is wrong. When the light goes on, he can't ignore it. He's got to pull the handle and initiate the sequence to manage the thoughts and behaviors filtered through those emotions or be burned up.

> Everyone who hears these words of mine and puts them into practice is like a wise man who built his house on the rock. The rain

came down, the streams rose, and the winds blew and beat against that house; yet it did not fall, because it had its foundation on the rock. (Matthew 7:24–25)

Translation: When emotions are swirling and negatively influenced perceptions are tossing you around, reach for the truth, hang on to it, walk in it, and let your emotions come *after* you've been obedient.

Remembering our identity in Christ and acting on it under pressure can be difficult, especially when emotional comfort is on the line. When we want something badly, we don't want to think. Satan knows this. That's why he wants you to *feel* your way into wrong actions versus *act* the right way into new feelings. Satan aggressively waits for men to give in to their emotions because he knows they will be as unreliable and inconsistent as those emotions *and* as easy to control. When you are low, he wants you to attach to the perception created by your emotions that all is lost, all is fatal and final. God, on the other hand, says, "I am with you in the valley of the shadow of death, no need to fear, I will walk you through this. Painful, yes, but also purposeful and productive for you."

Mismanaging emotions is like escorting a group of known terrorists into a large international airport, clearing them through security, and seating them in first class. Well-managed emotions are processed without special clearance and brought before the security stations of God and others. It requires humility, faith, and a commitment to growth. But you can be assured that Satan hates it when a man is in emotional control of himself, because it means only one thing.

Satan has lost control.

evil loves religion

Men never do evil so completely and cheerfully as when they
do it from religious conviction.

—BLAISE PASCAL

"Houston, we've had a problem."*

Astronaut James Lovell's famous expression is now synonymous with
any potentially huge tragedy. Yet it wasn't until I watched director Ron
Howard's film portrayal of the *Apollo 13* saga, starring Tom Hanks as
Lovell, that the expression came to life in its original context. To this
day, the film is one of my all-time favorite docudramas. A human drama
is one thing, but a real-life human drama unfolding in outer space before
a watching world is beyond unforgettable. It's immortal. Consider the
events:

---

* Though the movie changed the line, this is the actual quote.

- An oxygen tank explodes on the way to the moon. Lovell delivers his line: "Houston, we've had a problem."
- Instead of landing on the moon, the crew must now leave the main service module, which has lost all its oxygen because of the explosion, and use the lunar module (LM) as a lifeboat, since its oxygen stores were intact. In what NASA engineers call a free-return trajectory, they will go around the back of the moon so its gravitational pull can slingshot the spacecraft back to Earth.
- Because flight controllers did not know how much damage the service module had sustained, they decided to attempt a high-risk course correction of the spacecraft using the engine of the lunar module.
- Within hours of the accident the first of two engine firings were initiated to accelerate the spacecraft's return to Earth. Later, it was determined that a second firing was necessary because the spacecraft was getting off course. This is when the rescue mission hit the biggest of its many obstacles to getting home safely.

The description of what happened next comes directly from the *Apollo 13* lunar surface journal for the mission:

> The first burn went smoothly and there was every reason to believe that the LM engine would function perfectly the second time as well. However, for this second burn, the crew had to take particular care to make sure that the engine was pointed in just the right direction and, because of the accident, they had to deal with some unusual navigation problems. Because they were traveling through vacuum, there was nothing to disperse the cloud of Service Module debris that enveloped the spacecraft. As they peered through the LM's one-power telescope trying to make star sightings, glints of sunlight reflecting off the debris made the job all but impossible. And to add to their difficulties, they were all exhausted and kept

making uncharacteristic mistakes. But they kept at it and, with help from the ground, figured out how to use sightings of the Sun and the crescent Earth to verify their alignment and then did the job over and over to make sure that they had it right. When the time came, the burn was perfect.

On 17 April 1970 at 12:07:44 p.m. Central Standard Time, the crew of Apollo 13 splashed down only 4 miles from the prime recovery ship.[1]

Did you catch that? They were *eyeballing* the earth and sun to figure out exactly when and how long to execute the second burn! When you watch the movie, you are transported inside that lunar module and forced to feel the pressure surrounding that second burn. If it is just a little off, they rocket past Earth into an abyss from which they will never return.

It makes you hold your breath.

A Little Off

Amazingly, in our fight, it's possible for even the inertia created by our salvation to be manipulated and thrown off course. Though we might fully embrace the gospel and God's power in our lives, slight trajectory and velocity changes of the mind, over enough time, can pull our vessels way off course.

I know. It doesn't seem fair.

> Satan makes well-calculated attempts to take advantage of our spiritual passion and momentum to slingshot us toward his own target of a synthetic *"Christian"* life.

And it isn't. But just like the imperiled space capsule had to fire its engines at exactly the right times to keep the right trajectory, God's man must employ constant vigilance to listen to the right voices and use the indicators to steer toward an authentic, Christ-centered life. Satan makes well-calculated attempts to take advantage of our spiritual passion and momentum to slingshot us away from God's highest purposes and toward his own target of a *synthetic* "Christian" life. That target, as the name suggests, has the look of faith but none of its power.

Think about it. Have you seen this before? A Christian with good intentions in fact ends up spreading corruption through his self-serving "acts of service," never suspecting he's the least bit off track. It is possible for evil to masquerade as good under the cover of religion without the person even realizing he's doing wrong. Sure, he might wonder where his blessings are or sense there's something missing in his joy. But take a look at the next Fight Fact:

fight fact

Satan knows that good intentions, just a little off, can cause significant damage. He loves to Trojan-horse evil using God's people as the vehicles. And the result ends up doing more harm than good.

What if I were to tell you that I was one of these Christians? I was what you might call a liquid-hydrogen convert to Christianity—as in WARNING: HIGHLY FLAMMABLE MATERIAL. If you have ever bumped into anyone who's "seen the light," you know what I'm talking about—very excited, very passionate, tons of energy, and fully committed (practically needing to *be* committed). That was me—all jacked up and "*en fuego.*"

For many, I'm sure, the label *wack job* would have fit. Some of my friends who witnessed my initial transformation could confirm that I was

definitely not ashamed to be called a Christian, and I was naively confident that I had all the answers now that I was on the winning team of
the Savior and the sword.

I felt things too. I was *thrilled* to be going to heaven. I was *overjoyed* that
my sins were forgiven. I was *over the moon* about my purpose for the first
time in my life. I owned an identity that was positively glorious—I was a
Christian. It was quite a momentum shift for a guy whose classmates
voted him Life of the Party. With one life-altering decision, a major
explosion of passion and purpose had erupted within me. That was the
upside.

The other, highly volatile side of me contained the accelerant material
I hoped my newfound faith would magically erase. These were the unstable elements lurking in my character: patterns of thinking, mixed
motives, emotional injuries in need of healing, deep insecurities, fears,
longings, disappointments, shame, discontentment, and a deep-rooted
need for approval and acceptance. God wanted to work those out His
way over time, but what I didn't know was that Satan wanted a shot at
them too. And with *me, a signed-and-sealed Christian!* How could he
possibly touch me?

Jesus' words to His disciples tell the whole story: "Make sure that the
light you think you have is not really darkness" (Luke 11:35, NLT 1996).

Whoa. Hold on.

The Devil can't take away our salvation or connection to Jesus. True. But
he can still do his best to make that connection as unhealthy and toxic as
possible. His aim with me was simple: take an authentic conversion and
attempt to make it shallow, synthetic, and full of contradictions.

How? First, he used the residual emotional, mental, and character issues still inside me to fashion a security blanket of faith around the broken parts of my manhood—the parts that made anything they touched self-centered, dysfunctional, and prone to sin. Second, he encouraged me to express my old character traits, the ones created by my flesh and the world under the guise of my new faith. I experienced the fast track of acceptance, affirmation, and approval for my *en fuego* faith, my Bible knowledge, my wise opinions, my powerful prayers, my Bible-study leadership, my mission trips, and my passionate witnessing. Satan took me by the neck and got me doing all the right things with mixed motives.

Third, he made me religious. Today, I imagine Satan telling his emissaries something like, "Listen up, fiends. You've got plenty to work with up there on that one. So no blatant stuff. Just suggest a few little attachments, get him feeling good. That should pull the lad way off." He set things up for them and then delivered his plan, the plan to destroy *me:*

- Get him focused on performance. He'll overperform because he's a pleaser and a competitor.
- Get him self-righteousness. Get him to start taking the credit for his own goodness versus crediting the work of the Cross and giving God the glory. Spiritual pride is as good a pride as any.
- Cause him to worry. About what doesn't matter: maintaining his image, getting approval, being liked, being the best, whatever. Get him thinking he's the perfect Christian so he'll forget the internal character changes and focus on external behaviors.
- Create a public-private split. Convince him to be himself in private and super-Christian in public. And tell him he can never talk about it.
- Create a false sense of security in what he's doing for God versus who he is in God. When he messes up, convince him that it's *all* his fault and that he needs to work harder. Maybe he'll throw in the towel.

- Make him think he's the only one. Tell him Christians never struggle with his kind of flaws and temptations. The longer he hides his true self, the higher the wall will become. Maybe he'll be miserable enough to go back to old coping habits.
- Encourage him to think negatively about the world to feel better about himself. Convince him he's justified in being judgmental and he'll appear narrow-minded, ignorant, and blind to the real needs of people, alienating him from the world.
- Use his faith to cultivate a false sense of control and authority.

Those were Satan's tactics to throw me from my trajectory for Christ into a radically different orbit. If successful, what you'd see is a good God's man going bad.

When I converted to Christianity, there was never a discussion among Satan and his agents lamenting or complaining that they had "lost another one" to Jesus. On the contrary, *real evil* is much more vigilant and intelligent. Satan can take the soft dough of our faith and twist it into a thing of harm. He is undaunted in his quest mainly because he has had such wild success sending people into a religious orbit.

My story is not unique. It's happened billions of times over: grace *is* sweet, especially to a wretch. Anyone who has encountered Christ's warm embrace of acceptance and affirmation *should* be *"en fuego."* At the same time, I absolutely gape at how quickly and easily my fresh and my newfound faith and beliefs were hijacked by conflicting desires, a deep need to be seen,

In short, I became goofy. And there's nothing goofier than a goofy Christian.

and a desperate need for approval. My momentum was hijacked and redirected by bad thinking. Mixed motives began to fuel my faith. I became a hypocrite and a horrible advertisement for Christianity in the early phases of my spiritual journey, harming the cause of Christ more than helping it.

In short, I became goofy. And there's nothing goofier than a goofy Christian.

Dysfunctional Spirituality

When Jesus saw goofy, He didn't hesitate to call it on the carpet. Let's study the film in Matthew 23:

> Woe to you, teachers of the law and Pharisees, you hypocrites! You give a tenth of your spices—mint, dill and cummin. But *you have neglected the more important matters* of the law—*justice, mercy and faithfulness.* You should have practiced the latter, without neglecting the former. You blind guides! You strain out a gnat but swallow a camel. (verses 23–24)

Translation: Look at yourselves! This must be rope-a-dope day for Satan! Good intentions, boys, but wrong target. He's made you all judgmental nitpickers. The spiritual life is not an accounting class.

> Woe to you, teachers of the law and Pharisees, you hypocrites! You clean the outside of the cup and dish, but inside they are full of greed and self-indulgence. Blind Pharisee! *First clean the inside* of the cup and dish, and then the outside also will be clean. (verses 25–26)

Translation: You've fallen for the oldest trick in the book. You *can't fake it.* Conviction without character is a C-A-T-A-S-T-R-O-P-H-E. Get this: no rearrangement of bad eggs can *ever* produce a good omelet. So start over!

Work it from the inside out, beginning with your motives. Find good ones, and then you'll get good results.

Jesus wants spiritual integrity. He wants talk *and* walk, belief *and* behaviors. You might bamboozle the public, but He sees the real you. Here's how He evaluates His men: "The LORD said to Samuel, 'Do not consider his appearance or his height, for I have rejected him. The LORD does not look at the things man looks at. Man looks at the outward appearance, *but the LORD looks at the heart*'" (1 Samuel 16:7). Character means more to God than conduct. One is what you're about. The other is what He's about.

Go back to the basics: "He has showed you, O man, what is good. And what does the LORD require of you? To act justly and to love mercy and to *walk humbly* with your God" (Micah 6:8).

Satan's goal is dysfunctional spirituality. He's working overtime to create inauthentic, judgmental, insecure, and insulated Christians so in love with *acting* "Christian" that they don't have a clue what it means to *be* one. They're uncomfortable around people who aren't Christians, they don't know how to engage them, and they make "spiritual" excuses for not connecting with them: they're bad influences, unrepentant, making bad choices. Should people who don't know Christ already know how to act like Him? Religious attitudes confuse people and kill our compassion.

People need grace, not goofy religion. Study film of Jesus engaging a "religious" guy and squeezing off a few rounds at his pride.

> *He wanted to justify himself,* so he asked Jesus, "And who is my neighbor?"
> In reply Jesus said: "A man was going down from Jerusalem to

Jericho, when he fell into the hands of robbers. They stripped him of his clothes, beat him and went away, leaving him half dead. *A priest* happened to be going down the same road, and when he *saw the man,* he *passed by on the other side.* So too, *a Levite,* when he came to the place and *saw him, passed by on the other side.* But a Samaritan, as he traveled, came where the man was; and when he saw him, he took pity on him. He went to him and bandaged his wounds, pouring on oil and wine. Then he put the man on his own donkey, took him to an inn and took care of him. The next day he took out two silver coins and gave them to the innkeeper. 'Look after him,' he said, 'and when I return, I will reimburse you for any extra expense you may have.'

"Which of these three do you think was a neighbor to the man who fell into the hands of robbers?"

The *expert* in the law replied, "The one who had mercy on him."

Jesus told him, "Go and do likewise." (Luke 10:29–37)

Translation: Religious guys don't understand the faith they claim. They are not neighbors. They are synthetic, shallow, and scared to reach out to people not like themselves. They are dysfunctional, appearing sane but acting goofy in the face of huge needs around them. In the end, it's about *them,* their agendas, and their convenience while people lie dying by the side of the road. They have "rules of engagement" that say to the outsider: you can meet me on my terms when it's convenient for me, but I refuse to *get messy.*

Real faith breaks all the rules of man to meet a need. Authentic faith abandons personal dignity to restore someone else's. Sincere faith means not being at peace until someone else's is secured. The Samaritan, according to Jesus, understands the fighting behaviors of a real God's man.

You can see why evil loves religion. In the end, the strongest, most convincing evil is the kind that masquerades as the perfect good. "With or without religion, good people can behave well and bad people can do evil," observes Nobel Prize–winning physicist Steven Weinberg, "but for good people to do evil—that takes religion." The interesting thing about this brilliant man is that he is not an atheist. He is, however, anti-Christianity because of the pimping of it by evil. He believes that throughout history, good-intentioned but slightly off expressions have led to malicious executions of "God's work" by those who claimed the name of Christ. He speaks for countless millions who have been encouraged to keep their distance from the Savior because Christians got pimped by evil and turned *religious.* Think the Crusades. Think slavery. Think ethnic cleansing. Think abortion-clinic bombings. Think religiously fueled hatred, sectarianism, church splits, and church infighting. Think prosperity gospel, which tells its adherents they're entitled to health and wealth if they just believe enough. Dysfunctional spirituality. All twisted religious "answers." All its expressions have leaders (mostly men), and all abuse people.

Satan's response: "Brilliant."

"Spiritual abuse is rather like any physical or sexual abuse," says U2 front man Bono. "It brings you to a place where you can't face the subject ever again. It's rare for the sexually abused to ever enjoy sex again. So, too, people who are spiritually abused by religion can rarely approach the subject of religion with fresh faith. They wince and twitch. My religious life has been trying to get through a minefield without coming out of it in a wheelchair. And I have. Well, okay, with a limp."[2] Religion distances people from a real relationship with a living and loving God and leaves survivors with a spiritual limp. In short, religion messes everything up.

In this incredibly high-stakes war, God's man must opt out of religion and jump into the real battle for the heart and soul. Man-made religion is war against man and God by satanic diversion. It takes the focus off the real Enemy and puts it on man, letting bad character corrupt a good thing. It's as useful a tool as murder, lust, adultery, and idolatry. Religion is synonymous with impotence, and Satan uses it to insulate believers against true spiritual advances.

Make no mistake, Satan wants to get you religious just like he did with me. As Charles Spurgeon reminds us, "There are a thousand razors with which the devil can shave off the locks of a consecrated man without his knowing it."

So how religious have you become? Are you distant from the real needs of those around you? If you're judgmental toward outsiders, afraid to get dirty, or "playing Christian" to feel better, rest assured that Satan is playing you. The way you fight this, Jesus says, is by simply being the good neighbor who walks humbly, acts compassionately, and loves mercy. If you are thinking these qualities are not manly, you're right. They're godly.

I know this has been tough, but if you've made it this far, you're finally ready to move into the arena of battle to engage evil. Don't feel the need to rush on if you sense you need some more time in these last few chapters first. There's a lot of info here to digest. But once you're ready, take a deep breath, and follow me into the next pages.

Part 3

engaging evil

fix bayonets!

Captain, my religious belief teaches me to feel as safe in battle as in bed. God has fixed the time for my death. I do not concern myself about that, but to be always ready, no matter when it may overtake me. That is the way all men should live, and then all would be equally brave.

—GEN. THOMAS "STONEWALL" JACKSON

The door shut behind us. I was now inside a pagan house of worship.

Earlier that morning we pulled into the remote village of San Juan Chamula after a two-hour drive from San Cristóbal, the capital of the state of Chiapas in southern Mexico. We were there to encourage a local pastor who was attempting to build a church and conduct a covert operation against evil in this town.

Having left the paved road, we were now amid the squalor and poverty of a rural, indigenous section of Mexican countryside. Shacks littered with signs of hard life and the ubiquitous smell of smoldering fires told us we were not in Kansas anymore, much less the comfort of our hotel many hours away. We were in another world—*their world.* We spotted them, and they spotted us. It was our first moment of confrontation.

There were no words, just glaring and contempt. The local mob bosses in these parts were called *caciques* (kah-SEE-kays) who literally policed these villages with their own brand of frontier justice. There were a dozen or so of them, stopping in their tracks and staring at our large van. More to the point, they were staring at us, studying us, and searching their minds for clues as to why a load of men they didn't know suddenly showed up from out of town *here.* What a show of testosterone: complete with white cowboy hats, black alpaca vests, and rugged cowboy boots. The only accessories missing were six-shooters on their hips and bandoliers of bullets across the shoulders. Apparently, the Wild West was still very much alive in the rural south of Mexico.

One of our local guides (our driver) was looking pretty unnerved, like he'd caught a sudden case of rheumatic fever. He was looking at the locals and struggling in vain *not to look at them* at the same time. It was the look of pure fear, and later that day I learned why. This same group had threatened to kill his dad and told the driver never to come back. His dad was a pastor.

And if the local authorities knew why I was there, whom I was with, and what I was doing, there was no telling what their reaction would be. I couldn't imagine what was going through our guide's mind, but their glaring eyes made my friend begin to sweat, swallow, and pray. These guys intimidate and kill pastors for sport without conscience or fear of consequence. In fact, one of our visits would include some time with the wife of a pastor who had been recently murdered. Caciques are the judge and jury in these parts, paranoid guys with a low tolerance for those who would threaten their traditional ways of living or the local religion. I speculated that the only thing keeping them from acting hostile toward us was the potential revenue they thought we might bring their local economy. For all they knew, we were tourists coming to visit their village square, unload way too many pesos on trinkets and crafts, snap some pictures in front of the "church," and be on our way.

At least, that's what we were hoping.

After visiting with our local pastor contact, unloading some needed supplies, and giving encouragement, we headed out of the back country and into the heart of darkness: the town square in San Juan Chamula. The moment we stepped from the van and walked into the market square toward the church, all of us felt spiritual darkness closing in on us.

The local mystics and pagan priests call this little village the "bellybutton" of the earth, a reflection of both the remoteness and the spiritism that pervades the culture here. There is a palpable deception lurking beneath the surface, an evil reality, a spiritual oppression that is sensed and felt. You feel like you are in an episode of *The Twilight Zone* where everything appears normal but *something's up*. You can't quite put your finger on it.

What you *see* are normal buildings, normal merchants, and normal behaviors that one would connect to any town square or tourist destination. What you *feel* is a void of real life, an emptiness, an oppression, a slavery of soul, and an evil pretense inspiring it all. *How ironic,* I thought. My mission was to play along with this farce and simulate the behavior of a conventional tourist—curious, inquisitive, and nonthreatening.

Then we spotted our target.

From all appearances, the outside of the building looked like many churches I had seen in Mexico: bright green and orange accents, Mission-style architecture, and very large wooden doors. Oddly, the local authorities formed a perimeter of wooden barricades about fifty yards in front of the entrance to create a "safety" zone around the building, making it easy to see the human traffic in and out. We were warned that the caciques strictly enforced the no-photo rule inside the "house of worship," so we gawked, pointed, and posed convincingly at the perimeter before entering the zone. Our cameras were checked at the door. And what came next was surreal.

The five of us had been told what we would see, but we were still emotionally unprepared. The sights and sounds are etched on my brain:

- Large statues of different icons and saints in cages with strings of lights draped over them. Their hollow expressions and sunken eyes accentuate the hopelessness in this house of worship.
- Pockets of people, twos and threes, parents with children, husbands with wives, and neighbors with neighbors, like zombies, swaying on a soft current, back and forth, back and forth, their eyes fixed like they're dead. No music, no sound but their moaning, but still they move, their faces drawn and expressionless.
- Candles, lots of them in front of each family. Tall and skinny, affixed by their own wax onto the floor, creating a private shrine for each family. I am careful not to hit them as I walk by.
- Blood sacrifices. Baby chicks are taken out small boxes, sliced, and offered to the spirits. These, too, must be purchased along with the alcohol. All the accessories keep our cacique friends flush with cash. No wonder they hate pastors.

Earlier we'd learned that all the worshipers would be drunk with a special brand of alcohol called *posh* made exclusively for worship in this temple. It is a whiskey-based drink, native to the indigenous Tzotzil, made from sugar cane juice and mixed with cola to make it drinkable. Families, including the children, commence their worship by drinking it, and they continue to drink it as they make their offerings. Even the kids. Every sensibility as a father of three rose up in me. I felt like I was in some Indiana Jones adventure, sneaking around in disguise amid great evil and attempting, against all odds, to sabotage what was going on around me.

For the next forty-five minutes, behind those closed doors, we acted like tourists but waged war like warriors. We may have appeared surrounded, outnumbered, and outflanked, but we were there to *fight*.

It was reminiscent of when fellow general Barnard Bee reported to Stonewall Jackson that they were being beaten back by the enemy at the battle of First Bull Run. Bee was in a panic. Upon hearing the report, Jackson calmly replied, "Then, sir, we will give them the bayonet." We did not panic either. Instead, we fixed bayonets.

Close Combat

Before going into this temple, I had talked to our team about what to do when inside. I told them to pair up, let their eyes register a target or situation, and then take it down in prayer. "Be specific, be bold, and don't stop firing in the name of Jesus." For me, this was a modern-day Jericho. Jesus' words flowed into my mind, making me even freer in the fight: "I have given you authority to trample on snakes and scorpions and to overcome all the power of the enemy; *nothing will harm you*" (Luke 10:19). I was paired up with Alan, and as we took everything in, we took aim and started squeezing off round after round after round.

My journal of this encounter gives the firsthand account of what I was thinking and praying from *inside* this temple of doom:

December 9, 2006, The Devil's House

It was a hot LZ. I never stopped firing. I prayed for the destruction of the building by an earthquake as an event that would speak to this people about God's displeasure and create an openness to a witness of the gospel. I claimed every life I encountered for Jesus, every wood beam, and every brick. Alan and I acted like we were pointing and commenting when, in fact, we were praying warfare prayers. I have never seen this kind of paganism, and yet Jesus was with Alan and me. We could sense His presence and covering like Daniel and his friends did in the flames of the fiery furnace.

We prayed against all powers, thrones, principalities, and evil raised up in this place against the knowledge of God. We prayed against the lies and bondage of these precious ones of God ("Woe to those who make my little ones stumble"). We asked for the destruction of all images and idols. We asked for God's kingdom to come. We asked for God to set these captives at our feet free. We prayed the Scripture from John 17:3: "That they may know you, the only true God, and Jesus Christ, whom you have sent." We prayed for every cacique's mind and for the destruction of strongholds and patterns of thought. We prayed for miraculous signs that would cut through culture and communicate God's power like nothing else. We declared the drunken before us for Jesus and not for evil, that they would drink a new wine of the Holy Spirit. We prayed the Scripture. We prayed truth. We prayed in His mighty name.

We attacked a heavily fortified position. We did not run. We fixed bayonets. We advanced. We fought in the flames. We embraced our mission. As we walked out of the building, we were still praying. The light of the sun was a stark contrast to the macabre glow of candles. The silhouettes of real human beings, living and breathing, a contrast to the lifeless gaze of the icons and zombies. And yet the air still felt heavy and rife with evil as we approached our last place of battle: a tall black statue of a traditionally dressed cacique with a bronze plaque. It read Autoridad Municipal.

"We prayed the Scripture. We prayed truth. We prayed in His mighty name."

Literally meaning (as you might have gleaned), "Municipal Authority." Functionally and culturally it is meant to communicate, "We are the law."

Uh-huh, right. That they have to have a bronze statue made and declare it tells the whole story. In my journal I wrote, "What a joke! They don't earn their authority through serving the people, they must manipulate, deceive, kill, and destroy to have influence. Jeff read from John 17 to put this all in perspective where Jesus prayed to his Father, 'You have given *Me* authority over all men.'" We prayed for that day when these "authorities" will meet the only true and real Cacique in the universe, hopefully sooner versus later. Then we got back into the van to go to our next field of battle.

In war, when a regiment is given an assignment to carry out a frontal assault across open ground or to take a hill, there is a pause *and* a quickening of the warrior. His duty is his alone. The consequences, if he is realistic, are in God's hands. All he knows is that he's getting called into close quarters with the enemy, and he needs to discharge his duty to his country, to the cause, and to his comrades.

This is the reality of every warrior. He knows he is called by God to combat evil, many times in close quarters, wherever he's been assigned. The field of battle is inconsequential. Whether he's in a remote village in southern Mexico, with the remote in his hand defending against a screen full of porn, or looking into the remote eyes of a lost soul, he brings his *all* to the battle.

He's called to fight that particular battle, or God wouldn't have placed him there. As long as he's breathing, he's fighting—right where he lives. God's man knows evil is swimming below the water lines of visible reality. His daily duty is to fix bayonets in personal fields of battle right *now.* His orders stand as follows until he is called home:

> Finally, be strong in the Lord and in the strength of His might. Put on the full armor of God, so that you will be able to stand firm against the schemes of the devil. For our struggle is not against flesh and blood, but against the rulers, against the powers, against the world forces of this darkness, against the spiritual forces of wickedness in the heavenly places. Therefore, take up the full armor of God, so that you will be able to resist in the evil day, and having done everything, to stand firm. (Ephesians 6:10–13, NASB)

The word "struggle" in my Greek New Testament is the word *palē* (PAW-leh). It means "all-out," hand-to-hand, foot-to-foot, wrestling/boxing match. In the first century, wars were not fought remotely by merely pushing buttons or from the air by firing missiles. There was only one kind of fighting—with muscles. The assumption is that God's man fights in close quarters against evil. Human effort is inadequate (*"be strong in the Lord and in the strength of His might"*), as are human means (*"Put on the full armor"*), if the man in the contest hopes to survive the encounter.

> *The assumption is that God's man fights in close quarters against evil.*

Flesh and blood may be the instruments of evil, but "powers," "world forces of this darkness," and "spiritual forces of wickedness" are the ones we're to attack, grapple with, and subdue by all spiritual means. This brand of fighting man is necessary if evil is to be uprooted.

When God leads His men out and orders them to fix bayonets, there is something inherently eerie that happens when the command is obeyed. In a spiritual sense, the sound of the cold metal sliding from the scabbard, the loud metallic *click* of the knife locking deeply into the rifle lug, bonding with its warrior, sends a chill through the enemy. It is a different sensation. Lots of men chamber rounds in rifles, but men seldom fix naked, sharp steel to them unless a struggle to the death is imminent, *one on one*. The sight of a regiment advancing with fixed bayonets has a withering psychological effect on the enemy.

> **fight fact**
> *You are the picture of this man ready to fight hand to hand, and it should be disturbing for our enemy to see you rising out of your bunker.*

Get the picture?

God's Sheepdogs

There are sheep. There's a Shepherd. There are wolves. And there are sheepdogs.

In his excellent book *On Combat*, Lt. Col. (Ret.) Dave Grossman highlights the distinctions between the sheep and sheepdogs in relationship to the wolves. It is a telling reminder that not all will choose to fight. But the called ones move to meet evil head-on. Grossman's reflections speak to the present condition of the church and our relationship to the Evil One. The italicized highlights below are Grossman's.[1]

1. *Most of the people in our society are sheep. They are kind, gentle, productive creatures who can only hurt one another by accident.* When it comes to the general character of the church and its men, evil sees sheep—mild, placid, calm, grazing.

2. *Then there are the wolves, and the wolves feed on the sheep without mercy. Do you believe there are wolves out there who will feed on the flock without mercy? You better believe it. The moment you forget that or pretend it is not so, you become a sheep.* There is no safety in denial. Part 1 of this book dealt with this head-on. Evil, Satan, and demons are not only real, intelligent, and intentional, they are also lethal to their targets. Bennett based his parable on Jesus talking about us and the Devil in the gospels.

3. *Then there are the sheepdogs, and I am a sheepdog. I live to protect the flock and confront the wolf. If you have no capacity for violence, then you are a healthy and productive citizen, a sheep. If you have a capacity for violence and no empathy for your fellow citizens, then you have defined yourself as an aggressive sociopath, a wolf. But what if you have a capacity for violence and a deep love for your fellow citizens? What do you have then? A sheepdog, a warrior, someone who is capable of walking into the heart of darkness, into the universal human phobia, and walking out unscathed.* Identity is a choice, an alignment of will, and a statement of purpose. An identity requires duty and responsibility to that identity. Choosing one's identity mitigates the fear connected with the duties he discharges. God's man is dangerous and good. An awesome combination. That was Jesus. That is us.

4. *The sheepdog disturbs the sheep. He is a constant reminder that there are wolves in the land. The sheep would much rather have the sheepdog*

cash in his fangs, spray-paint himself white, and say, "Baa." Until the wolf shows up; then the entire flock tries desperately to hide behind one lonely sheepdog. Read the story of Jephthah in Judges 11:1–10, the classic sheepdog who was needed and called home by the shepherd to be a fighting man. He was not made of their ilk, he was different, and he was skeptical of the sheep. God's man is not out to win popularity contests among the sheep. He's bent on one thing: dispossessing the wolf of his ability to harm the sheep.

5. **Understand that there is nothing morally superior about being a sheepdog; it is just what you choose to be.** *Also understand that the sheepdog is a funny critter: he is always sniffing around out on the perimeter, checking the breeze, barking at things that go bump in the night, and yearning for a righteous battle. Here is how the sheep and the sheepdog think differently. The sheep pretend the wolf will never come, but the sheepdog lives for that day.* By choosing to fight evil, God's man commits to discerning it. Part 2 of this book showed how to sniff the breeze. We talk about evil and rebuke it. We bark at what others might deem trivial, and we may disturb the "sleep" of other Christians, making them decide their own identities.

6. **If you want to be a wolf, you can be one,** *but the sheepdogs are going to hunt you down, and you will never have rest, safety, trust, or love.* Jesus Christ came for one reason: "The reason the Son of God appeared was to destroy the devil's work" (1 John 3:8). Make the connection: He lives in us, we fight in His character, and we've been handed His same mission on a variety of levels. We do not let evil rest on the beaches of our lives. We go after it with impunity.

7. **If you want to be a sheepdog and walk the warrior's path,** *you must make a conscious and moral decision every day to dedicate, equip, and prepare yourself to thrive in the toxic, corrosive moment when the wolf comes knocking at your door.* Look at the words: "conscious… decision…every day…dedicate…equip…prepare…thrive." I like the

last word the best. God's sheepdogs risk dedication (i.e., discipline) in the direction of their ultimate hope. "Share in suffering as a good soldier of Christ Jesus. No soldier gets entangled in civilian pursuits, since his aim is to please the one who enlisted him. An athlete is not crowned unless he competes according to the rules. It is the hardworking farmer who ought to have the first share of the crops. Think over what I say, for the Lord will give you understanding in everything" (2 Timothy 2:3–7, ESV). Soldiers, athletes, and farmers do the hard things when they don't feel like it because of their identities, loyalties, and connected duties. Why? To win the object of their hope. How? By risking daily discipline.

8. ***This business of being a sheep or a sheepdog is not a yes-or-no dichotomy.*** *It is not an all-or-nothing choice. On the one end is an abject, head-in-the-sand sheep, and at the other end is the ultimate warrior. Few people exist completely on one end or the other. Most of us live somewhere in between.* The Bible presents a picture of God's man as both dangerous and good, even as Jesus is presented as both in the Scriptures. He is the Lion of the tribe of Judah and the Lamb of God. The twist is that both identities are equally courageous and strong. Yes, a courageous Lamb willing to sacrifice itself and a confident King of kings riding hard and fast toward evil, sword drawn, with armies in tow. My prayer is, "Lord, more sheepdog and less sheep, please."

Study God's men throughout history, and you'll understand why it's both necessary and practical to be engaged in the fight against evil. Look at Israel during the lives of two of its best fighters: Moses and Joshua. Look at their activity and study their spiritual health, and you will quickly see a powerful fact shine forth: as the Israelites fight and battle for kingdom advance, they have *no time or energy for sin.*

Now study the times following this in the book of Judges, when they forgot their identity, laid down their swords prematurely, and blended in with the Canaanites. Israel strays from God and rebels against His lordship. Here's the point: When they *perceive* that all is well, all is not well with God's people. When God's people are free from war, they *sin*. The fight stimulates dependence, provides focus, and gobbles up ground. Less fight, more sin. More fight, less sin. It's that simple.

So, God's man, fix bayonets!

yield to wield

Please take note that Satan is not afraid of our preaching the
word of Christ, yet how very much he is in fear of our being
subject to the authority of Christ.

—WATCHMAN NEE

My first *and only* red card as a soccer coach was well deserved.

I'd had enough of the center referee and his bad calls, allowing clear
fouls and in the process, teaching young men that dirty play pays on
the pitch. He'd been getting under my skin the whole match, and it
didn't help that we were losing 1–0 in a play-off with our rival club.
I've coached hundreds of matches and watched hundreds more at
all levels, so when I see officiating that threatens the safety of my
players, I can get…well, a little *energetic.* As a coach in soccer, that
means you direct some verbal attention toward the object of your
disaffections—the dude with the whistle in his hand and the funny
uniform.

From the first whistle, I could see he was going to allow above-average physicality. I was fine with that. A good center referee in a soccer match doesn't have to blow his whistle a ton, just swiftly and judiciously when he sees things getting out of hand to show that some lines cannot be crossed if you are going to call it *fútbol*. The one thing about soccer is that the below-the-belt infractions are obvious and can't be hidden. For experienced referees, the calls are easy. In fact, English fans in London know the game so well, the crowd responds to the action, good or bad, *in unison*. And they're almost always spot on.

So when some boys on the other side decided to test the limits of our referee's preference for physical play by blatantly fouling my boys, I expected to hear the unmistakable voice of authority intervene. Instead, there was only silence. Okay. I sucked it up. But when another dirty play ensued, I thought, *Surely, that was obvious.* I quickly flashed a look to the referee, his arms extended straight out from his body, the no-foul sign.

Our sideline erupted. "Hey!" one dad said. Another dad was not so cordial and snapped, "You're missing a good game, Ref!"

I could feel my own volcanic magma welling up inside as I started shaking my head at the referee. I tried to calm down, but only a few minutes later, after another clear elbow by one of their players to one of my boys' guts and, again, no whistle, I reacted. Okay, I let him have my unvarnished opinion. I may have said something about how he needed to transfer to ultimate fighting and give up soccer. And I made sure he heard me.

Then it happened.

My guy won the ball and took off toward the goal on a breakaway. As he raced down the left side of the field, he was taken down from behind by a defender who saw an opportunity. The ultimate foul, this variety is treated as malicious and aggressively penalized by officials. You get a red card and are sent off the field, suspended from playing your next match. Think Zinedine Zidane of France head-butting the Italian player in the chest during the 2006 World Cup Final. It didn't matter why: he was out of there. These obvious violent reactions earn automatic consequences.

So what do you think happened at my game? Nothing!

Not only was I already fizzing with pent-up aggression, my guy was down on the grass. Our sideline was all over this ref like the proverbial white on rice, and his face was starting to change to that color. Because he hadn't blown the whistle right away, he was now in that awkward place known as the point of no return. It was too late. Even if he'd wanted to change his mind now, he couldn't. There was no replay button to push. At that point, he had to stick by his call and dig in because fessing up would lose him all credibility.

Unfortunately, at this point, defending a murderer with prints on the weapon would have been easier. So I did what any angry dad and leader of the team does when his boy has just gotten murdered in front of his dearest friends and relatives: I proceeded to rip the ref a new pie hole.

"What game are you watching?" I yelled, running onto the field to attend to my player, who was still down. Did I mention, it was *loud*? "Unbelievable! This is unbelievable!"

Repeat this four times, bake it at five hundred degrees, and you'll begin to feel the special feelings I had for this referee. It was at this point that I stopped caring if I got thrown out of the game. I wanted him to *never* forget me and, hopefully, get so uncomfortable he'd throw in his whistle for good. That would be the only justice I could accept.

After we cleared the field and resumed play, I kept peppering the guy with my unbridled opinions of his officiating skills, including among other things the words "kindergarten," "blind," and "my mother." I was not apologetic. The freeze frame of my guy in a crumpled mass on the grass wasn't letting me go, and I didn't want it to let go of him either.

I just wanted to share the *love.*

After about fifteen minutes of this staccato tongue-lashing, he warned me. "That's enough, Coach." I couldn't help myself. Now *I* was the one at the point of no return, and my smart-aleck pills were kicking in. That means I interpreted "enough" to mean "more." I wanted a piece of him. So I muttered something under my breath about how he needed to find another sport to referee. He was waiting for that. *"Bleeeeeeeeeep!"* He whistled to stop play, reached into his pocket, yanked his red card, and saluted me in front of the crowd, telling me to leave the field.

> *I wanted a piece of him.*

By then, I was ready to leave. And so I did, compliant on the outside, but inwardly defiant.

Looking back, *I* know I was right. He should have felt guilty. I had the truth on my side. He was deluded. Those are the indisputable facts. But in the end, it didn't matter. *He* was the referee. I was the coach. *He* was in charge of that whistle, and I controlled nothing. *He* was vested with authority; *I* was invested in my cause.

To be perfectly clear: I did *not* obey the man. I obeyed *the uniform.* He was a frog the federation had turned into a prince.

He had the high ground.

The High Ground

In battle, you always want to be the one on the high ground. Whether in hand-to-hand combat or attacking as a unit, the decided advantage goes to the ones above. Yet when fighting evil, the high ground is not gained by physical action; it's a perception of your identity and *the authority behind it.* "Every *child of God* defeats this evil world, and we achieve this victory *through our faith.* And who can win this battle against the world? Only *those who believe* that Jesus is the Son of God" (1 John 5:4–5, NLT 2004).

If there is one thing Satan does not want you to internalize about yourself, it is this: *your royal identity gives you powerful authority.* Father, Son, and Holy Spirit *coming through a God's man* demand compliance from all. Satan holds no red card. He's no referee. He *can direct tactics* for his players on the field, but he *can't rule.* And he can hate it all he wants that a frog like me or you gets to wield the power, but he and the rest of his troops must respond to the authority of an officially endorsed and approved God's man.

Get this: *you* have been given the high ground, my brother.

Let this sink in: your identity in Christ gives you victory. Say it, my brother. You are a victorious warrior *in Christ*. "No, in all these things we are more than conquerors through him who loved us" (Romans 8:37). Declare your identity. No matter what battle you are facing, no matter what obstacle you are encountering, and no matter what feeling you are battling, *stop fighting the battles Satan has already lost and enjoy the victory*

> *Your royal identity and royal authority are a royal pain for Satan.*

Christ has already won. You may have forgotten this, neglected it, been kept in the dark about it, made blind to it, or simply compartmentalized it away into a theological box. But the reality remains.

Your royal identity and royal authority are a royal pain for Satan. That's the good news. But what many Christians forget is that this position of authority doesn't work unless we surrender completely.

Because the spiritual high ground in our war against evil is not a physical location but a spiritual condition, it means that there are conditions God requires of us to use *His* authority effectively. Remember the John Orr story. Intellectually, he flew through the application process, but he was rejected by the psychological exam. His profile as a narcissist raised chain-of-command issues, and the last thing LAPD or any law-enforcement agency wants is a rogue officer who abuses his authority.

> **fight fact**
> *God's man has no authority unless he is under authority. Full power and authority are given only to sons who have released full control of their lives to Jesus Christ.*

What does that look like for God's man? Let's study more film.

"Say the Word"

There is something about understanding authority that assures God when He approves His representatives. His willingness to advance His authority through a man depends on the man's willingness to accept His authority.

King Saul

"God removed Saul and replaced him with David, a man about whom God said, 'I have found David son of Jesse, a man after my own heart. He will do everything I want him to do'" (Acts 13:22, NLT 2004). The key words here are "removed" and "replaced." The transactional phrase is "everything I want him to do." Saul was removed because he obeyed God selectively, when it was convenient. Saul got into the bad habit of "mostly obeying," but David demonstrated that he understood God's overriding authority. Saul was ineffective because he hadn't surrendered.

King Asa

"The eyes of the LORD search the whole earth in order to strengthen those whose hearts are fully committed to him. What a fool you have been! From now on you will be at war" (2 Chronicles 16:9, NLT 2004). Asa was a good king, but his effectiveness in battle was compromised because he could not surrender full control of his life to God. There was a trust issue in play. When God told him to go for it, he did, but his eyes drifted off of God and onto the enemy. His faith was replaced by fear, and fear moved him to hire mercenaries to help him win his battles. God was offended, and Asa stopped winning.

Jesus

"I can do nothing on my own. I judge as God tells me. Therefore, my judgment is just, because I carry out the will of the one who sent me, not my own will" (John 5:30, NLT 2004). Jesus was placed over all because He was under the Father. His divinity and humanity blended functionally with humility and authority. All over the gospels He is found saying things like, "I only speak as the Father tells Me," "My food is to do the will of Him who sent Me," or, "I always do what pleases Him." (See John 8:28; 4:34; and 8:29.) This posture before God is coupled right alongside His position assigned by God: a position of authority. That's why He can command demons and commission men. That's why He can say, "All authority in heaven and on earth has been given to me. Therefore go and make disciples…. And surely I am with you always, to the very end of the age" (Matthew 28:18–20). Jesus showed us the linkage of submission and power for God's man.

The Roman Centurion

" 'I did not even consider myself worthy to come to you. But say the word, and my servant will be healed. For I myself am a man under authority, with soldiers under me. I tell this one, "Go," and he goes; and that one, "Come," and he comes. I say to my servant, "Do this," and he does it.' When Jesus heard this, he was amazed at him, and turning to the crowd following him, he said, 'I tell you, I have not found such great faith even in Israel.' Then the men who had been sent returned to the house and found the servant well" (Luke 7:7–10). It all coalesces in this scene with a man who is not yet even a follower of Christ. Go figure: a man who fights for a living *gets it*. In his world, submission to authority and the exercise of authority are inseparable. His men respond because they are under him and, at the same time, placed over others to exercise his authority.

The key phrase: "Say the word." Those words made the Son of God's jaw drop in utter astonishment. It was like He was looking for someone, anyone, who really understood Him, and He found His man in a soldier—a man who is under authority in order to exercise authority. "Say the word" says

- I know you are in charge.
- I know you are capable.
- I am not in control; you are in control.
- I am yielded to you.
- I have no power.
- You possess all power in my life at this moment.
- I am dependent on your will being done in my life.
- You are over me.

Find a great spiritual warrior, and I will show you ruthless submission to the will of God in that man's life. A rebuke of evil from a God's man who is unsurrendered or compart-mentalized, or who has mixed motives, is like an attack on a navy destroyer with a squirt gun—ill-advised. God knows the condition of our submission and refuses to chamber rounds of His power and authority in a man where there's a lack of spirit-ual integrity.

fight fact

Yielding to God's authority in your life *green-lights the wielding of His authority* through your life.

Even worse for *that* man is that evil can smell an actor. Look at this rare footage in the book of Acts involving well-intentioned men who had the right motive but the wrong life:

> Some Jews who went around driving out evil spirits tried to invoke the name of the Lord Jesus over those who were demon-possessed. They would say, "In the name of Jesus, whom Paul preaches, I

command you to come out." Seven sons of Sceva, a Jewish chief priest, were doing this. One day the evil spirit answered them, "Jesus I know, and I know about Paul, but who are you?" Then the man who had the evil spirit jumped on them and overpowered them all. He gave them such a beating that they ran out of the house naked and bleeding. (Acts 19:13–16)

Ouch. Would they *know* you?

Yielding and Wielding

Our visibility to evil is proportionate to the level of our obedience to God.

While writing the bulk of this manuscript, I was traveling and conducting conferences around the United States and Canada. Every weekend from the end of August to the middle of November was spent away from my family, on the road and in hotels. I chose to do this out of obedience to God, not because of the adventures of travel or even the honor of being asked by people to come. God asks, I pack my bags, and I go.

> *Our visibility to evil is proportionate to the level of our obedience to God.*

Many of you know exactly how this feels. It is challenging physically, emotionally, and spiritually. Traveling to minister is an obedience issue, not a preference issue. I would prefer to be home. I would prefer to sleep in my own bed. I would prefer to go to my kids' soccer games. But in my life and our family, convictions trump preferences. My family says they "tithe me to the Lord," and it's a battle for all of us to obey.

Perhaps this is why I was attacked that night.

Lafayette, Louisiana. I was sound asleep in a hotel when a hateful presence filled the room and caught me in a strong grip. It was so strong, it woke me up. Still lying down on my side but fully awake and conscious, I felt someone or something trying to hurt me physically. I had felt this type of oppressive and dark presence before on the mission field and when writing books. They wanted a shot at me just like they wanted a shot at Peter to sift him, and I am convinced Jesus *allowed* this to happen. He gave the okay to engage me.

Demons were allowed to attack my mind with hate-filled speech, and Satan allowed their presence to be felt all around me like a blanket of lead. It was straight out of a sci-fi film or a Harry Potter movie, but it was being played out *in real life* in this hotel room while I was ministering and writing this book.

My reaction was different than I might have expected: *I got angry.* I responded with a full awareness of what was going on and who was behind this, and I exerted over these demons my identity and authority as a servant of the living God. The words flooded out of me with full conviction.

Still lying down on my side, I extended my hand and firmly said, "Get out! Get out of here right now in the name of the Lord Jesus Christ. I am a servant of the living God, and I rebuke you in the name of Jesus Christ. I am covered by His blood, and you have no authority in this place. The Lord rebukes you. Go! Go to the place where Jesus tells you."

I kept at it for about fifteen minutes. The words just kept flowing. Finally, suddenly, I felt the presence lift. The ambush was over as fast as it began. It was replaced by a physical and spiritual sensation I've felt only a few times in my life: a pervading calm and tangible sense of the Lord's powerful presence and love. It's the feeling that comes when your heart finally gets the message from your head that it's over.

These evil emissaries were no match for a Spirit-filled man personally under God, the body of Christ, and pastoral authority. I knew how hard I was working to stay obedient to God in all areas. I knew I was working as hard as ever on my connection with Chrissy. I knew I was mentally pure. I knew I had no secrets. I was accountable. While fatigued and drained, I was being obedient in the ministry and giving to the men in Louisiana every ounce of insight and wisdom God's Word had provided. I knew I was fully armed and loaded. More important, *the demons knew that I knew.* This knowledge of my own submission gave me confidence and a holy aggression I'd never experienced before.

But *this* was different. I didn't know how good it would feel afterward. Yes, obedience and victories are meant to feel good. To be fully surrendered and fully usable in a fight against evil, *that* felt great. But I'd just repelled a tangible force of evil, and I knew I must have been doing something *very right* to get such attention. It also showed me that I'm not giving them anything to work with inside me, because they had to ask and get permission to attack me directly. It was a frontal assault designed to frighten me off—but it backfired. And what's greater, God knew it would. In the end, it all only served to stiffen my resolve, strengthen my awareness, and give me the battlefield test to pass along to you. The lesson that experience drove home was this: *my identity requires integrity to transact authority.*

Integrity and authority are inextricably linked.

God's man has an infinite power to wield. But to do it, he needs to *yield.* God knows it when He sees it. So does Satan. Practically, this means dealing with the footholds in your life, those areas of behavior or character where permission or power is given to Satan to traffic in darkness. Willingly striving to eliminate footholds is synonymous with increased personal power over evil.

Identifying these areas is not hard. They are the areas that harm your relationships with God and people on a consistent basis. God's man goes after *those areas* now by yielding to a *strong step of repentance* in each area. Here's how:

- announcing your opposition to evil in prayer out loud
- asking God to show you areas of your life where you do not like or want His authority. Ask Him, Where is there tension over Your control in my life? Where am I unwilling to go? What process am I resisting? Write down on paper what comes to mind.
- accepting responsibility for that tension and admitting that sin to God and to others
- affirming God's presence and His blessings in your life and submitting yourself to His total authority
- asking Him if there's anyone you harbor bitterness or resentment toward, confessing the sin of unforgiveness, and releasing that person for what he or she has done
- disciplining your mind by ordering it according to God's Word, committing it to aggressive management, and loving God with your thought life
- declaring war against any habitual sin by inspecting it with the light of His Word. Seeing it for what it is: sin. Owning it and amputating it from your life (read Mark 9:43–47 for the protocol). And your lifestyle is permanently, visibly altered.

Footholds can be small, but when left unaddressed they can grow. All the behaviors above reflect a change of mind, an awareness of reality and truth, and a response consistent with your identity in Christ. More to the point, these are *fighting behaviors* that send a strong and clear message that you possess a new commitment to being *under* God's authority to be a better steward *of* His authority.

The high ground in the fight against evil is authority.

Yield to wield.

armed and extremely dangerous: part one

The courage of a soldier is heightened by his knowledge of his profession, and he only wants an opportunity to execute what he is convinced he has been perfectly taught. A handful of men, inured to war, proceed to certain victory, while on the contrary numerous armies of raw and undisciplined troops are but multitudes of men dragged to slaughter.

—Flavius Vegetius Renatus, *De Re Militari,* AD 390

How did I wind up halfway around the world in a police station about to be interrogated by a KGB officer?

This was not how I thought my day would be going. Honestly, it had started innocently enough. My "North Star" team (Matt, Scott, and Tom) exited the hotel to link up with a camera crew who'd been sent to film us doing evangelism behind the iron curtain in communist lands. The video was going to be used to recruit other young sheepdogs to sign up for what we were doing. The resort town of Sochi, situated on Russia's Black Sea, was our last stop as covert tourists traveling the USSR as students looking to learn more about the culture.

That was the line we were using anyway.

Our "cultural exchanges" in the other cities we visited somehow always drifted to the topic of religion, faith, and spirituality. Go figure. In visits to Moscow, Yerevan (the capital of Armenia), and Almaty (in Kazakhstan), we had managed to help some of our new friends meet our Father, and we exchanged materials. To this point, it had been an adventure, a risky experience made more exciting by the fact that we were being followed most of the time. We were playing cat and mouse with low-level KGB tails everywhere we went.

But like all roller-coaster rides, there is that final turn and straight section of track where the air brakes puff and hiss and you start slowing down to disembark. That was us in Sochi. We had been running on adrenaline, our spiritual heart rates were beginning to slow down, and all that was left was to give an interview of our exploits on camera *in* country. Needless to say, the mood was up as we departed the hotel after breakfast. Mind you, we were still very aware that we might be followed as Americans, but we had come this far without incident and were thinking we had the system figured out.

We were wrong.

We ate breakfast and headed out to the coastline for a stroll to take pictures and shop. This day, instead of praying for people to meet and talk to, we were rendezvousing with a film crew who were also trying to be inconspicuous. After twenty minutes we spotted the group and followed them to a location they'd picked out to film these interviews. We sat down on a bench between two simple one-story structures that appeared to belong to a school.

In short order, the camera was set up in a hidden position, and the interviews began. For effect, everyone needed to answer the first question with, "I am in the Soviet Union right now, and we have just been to Moscow, Yerevan, and Alma-Ata." We were supposed to look like we were having a regular conversation. The camera was handheld below eye level.

About midway through the first interview I noticed several older people peering at us from inside the buildings. It happened three or four times, but it wasn't enough to alarm us. Then one older woman, about four feet tall and dressed in a robe and slippers, stepped outside to get a closer look at us. That's when it hit us that this might not be the best place to film our interviews. But it was already too late.

About thirty seconds later two police officers accompanied by two men in white suits from the school (it was actually a sanitarium for the mentally ill) came walking down the alley toward us. We tried to stay calm, but we were about to soil our shorts. All of us were now praying for deliverance from what we knew would be an extended visit with the police.

In today's Russia this would have amounted to nothing. But back in the pre-Gorbachev era of hard-line communism, six

> *We tried to stay calm, but we were about to soil our shorts.*

out-of-place Americans caused a commotion. The country had been under the evil grip of state-imposed atheism for nearly seventy years and did not take kindly to Westerners seeking to undermine their way of life.

gaging evilment>

None of us were talking, but *all of us* were praying for deliverance. This could be really bad.

We were escorted to a local police station and asked to sit down and wait. About ten minutes later, a stocky, heavyset man came in with a newspaper under his arm. He flashed a look over at the uniforms, who made a quick exit, and then, as if on cue, threw his newspaper onto the table next to us. When it hit the table, a large *thud* betrayed its contents, and it unfurled. All our eyes fell onto a Glock nine-millimeter automatic pistol.

If he was hoping for effect, he had our attention. This was *not* the principal's office. Fortunately, only one of us spoke fluent Russian, so it fell to him to have the first one-on-one with Glock-man. He grabbed his gun and waved my teammate Scott into another room for questioning. Thank God we had jettisoned all our *materials* in the three other cities. No hard evidence we were doing anything wrong.

We'd received a little training on what to say in the event we got pulled in for questioning. But until the moment arrives, you never know how you'll respond. The whole time I was thinking about Paul and Silas in that Philippian jail. They were doing stuff they weren't supposed to be doing in a foreign environment and got hauled in. But instead of giving in to fear, they were "praying and singing hymns to God" (Acts 16:25). They kept battling.

Since we were not behind bars as yet, we didn't break into song, but we did break into prayer, asking for the same kind of miraculous deliverance. After about twenty minutes of questioning, the sound of chairs being pushed back could be heard, followed by steps toward the door, and then the doorknob turned. Out stepped Scott and the KGB guy. He looked at the three of us and simply said, *"Svodnya"* (suh-*voad*-nee-ya). "Free."

We were free to go. Can you say *catharsis*? We were not chained, but just like in Acts, we felt the doors fly open, and we virtually floated out of that station. Needless to say, the North Star '85 group will be telling that story to our grandchildren. And for them, the story will be even more adventurous and spellbinding because of what we discovered upon returning home.

A few weeks later, back in California, we all met again. Of course, we couldn't help but relive our urban legend of being held at gunpoint in a KGB office. Almost as an afterthought, Matt added that his mom had been jolted out of a deep sleep that night at 3:00 a.m., burdened to pray for him.

"No way, so did mine," Tom said.

"That's weird, mine too," Scott chimed in.

My mom must have gotten in late from bingo at St. Joseph's or something, because she *didn't* wake up. But it was definitely a strange common denominator with the moms. And it could have ended right there, but Tom had the wherewithal to ask, "What night did she say that was?" All three moms had written it down. When we matched up our journals, the times and dates matched *perfectly*—down to the hour we were in that police station! I kid you not.

Apparently, God's cavalry was laying down cover fire to liberate the sheepdogs from the wolves.

And, yes, my children *do* know that story. My prayer is their children will know it too. It's a testimony to how God's power is exercised through His people. Our kids need to know that what Satan intends for evil, God can turn around for good. The spiritual battle is not fantasy or some story line for nice fiction. We have real weapons at our disposal, and like the old song goes, they can "open prison doors and set the captives free."

Above all, I want my kids to be challenged to wage the war of a Christian and do battle. "We are human, but we don't wage war with human plans and methods. We *use* God's mighty weapons, not mere worldly weapons, to knock down the Devil's strongholds" (2 Corinthians 10:3–4, NLT 1996). I want them to know that a Christian is never out of the fight, because he has weapons that are lethal beyond this world.

Mighty weapons of divine power to demolish evil. Isn't that every man's dream? You would think.

Know Your Weapons?

The Bible teaches that God's weapons were created to be used. *Used.* Versus what? Indulge me here:

- used versus *talked about*
- used versus *ignored*
- used versus *studied*
- used versus *debated*
- used versus *avoided*
- used versus *preached*
- used versus *misused*
- used versus *passed over*

I don't mean to rant about this, but far too often we men like to think of ourselves as Christ-loyal, but we don't want to use our weapons.

If we were to be graded on our familiarity with our weapons, like they do in any good standing army, I shudder to think what our spiritual instructors would say. "*How long* have you been a believer, boy?" Can you see it? Would that be you? The Bible assumes we'll actually *use* the weapons issued to *us*. I wouldn't be so sardonic if I weren't training men around the world to use God's weapons, having to first *acquaint them* with the very concept. As a trainer, it's downright embarrassing. But that ignorance and the healthy shame it produces pay off in competence and confidence. Don't *you* want a shot at "knocking down the Devil's strongholds"?

Let me put it this way: what do old war veterans talk about when they get together? The battles that defined them. Why is their bond so strong? Same. Now ask yourself: what is it you're really missing in your life that would create this kind of bond? And how do you think you'll get there? Right—fighting battles.

Well, my brother, you can't fight a battle against evil unless you're intimate with God's weapons. And we'll have an eternity to swap stories together, so let's start talking about how to use these babies in our fight against evil.

Satan wants to keep you from becoming adept with any one of these.

Know Your Position in Christ

As we've seen, knowledge of evil and of your position in Christ is the first weapon used in this fight. Not only does Satan try to keep intelligence and awareness about himself limited or misguided, he has the same objectives with your spiritual position and *the authority it commands*. Just saying "I am in Christ" is a blow to him. That identity and union, once internalized, activate your authority. It's the key that unlocks the door to spiritual power.

"I pray also that the eyes of your heart may be enlightened in order *that you may know* the hope to which he has called you, the riches of his glorious inheritance in the saints, and *his incomparably great power for us who believe.* That *power* is like the working of his *mighty strength,* which he *exerted* in Christ when he raised him from the dead and seated him at his right hand in the heavenly realms, far *above all* rule and authority, power and dominion, and every title that can be given, not only in *the present age* but also in the one to come" (Ephesians 1:18–21). Why does Paul pray for this, and why does Satan try to prevent that understanding from happening? It's a *power* issue, and the one who stands to lose power is not you, it's him! "That you may know" what? Answer: that your *total* identification and *total* spiritual union in Christ position you *for power against Satan.* The Devil cannot stand the thought of your wielding rule, power, authority, and dominion in Christ over evil *now,* "in the present age."

So, God's man, when you get a chance, tell him like you mean it, and mean it as you say it: "I am in Christ. My identity has been eclipsed. I have been deputized with full authority. I personally acknowledge, accept, and appropriate that authority in Jesus' mighty name." Say it often to remind yourself and Satan that you know who you are, and he should know it well. Your awareness of your spiritual identity is the basis, the power cell, for all other weapons.

Pray in Christ's Name

When I meet men in the community and invite them to our weekly men's meeting, I tell them, "Come this Thursday morning, and I'll buy you breakfast. Just tell them, 'Pastor Kenny is treating me to breakfast this morning,' and you'll be good to go." My name is all they need to say at the chow line because it stands for *my position* and *my authority* as a pastor in my church.

Requests authorized by Jesus are honored when you pray in His name. God's man speaks against the forces of darkness in a language *they understand.* When in doubt, just say the name. When confused, conflicted, or harassed, say the name. You don't have to be fancy, just throw it straight. If you affirm His *valid lordship* and your connection to Him, there is *valid authority* from His name. End of story. Use the weapon specifically and swiftly: "I rebuke all evil in this situation in the name of the Lord Jesus Christ." The key is to be simple, clear, and confident in your identity and connection to Christ.

But let me issue a warning: praying the name is *not* a magic wand. Just like the guys I buy breakfast for, allowing them to use my name, the question for God's man must be, "What is the *quality* of my connection to Christ?" It's a reference point for the request that either makes sense of it or diminishes it. In this sense, God's man does not need more authority in Christ, he needs *more intimacy with Christ* to make his authority *work.*

> *God's man does not need more authority in Christ,* he needs **more intimacy with Christ** *to make his authority work.*

If the connection you have with Jesus is real, current, and authentic, then you have freedom and confidence to pray in His name. That's why Jesus said, "Until now you have not asked for anything in my name. Ask and you will receive, and your joy will be complete" (John 16:24). Ask yourself, "How's my intimacy with Jesus?" Then go for it in His name, or repent and then go for it from the place of authentic relationship. If the relationship is solid, so will the nature of the request be.

Good intimacy produces good asks. Good asks win good fights.

Comply with Your Conscience Quickly

Your conscience is a front-line missile defense system installed by God for your fight against evil. It's sophisticated spiritual radar: "The lamp of the LORD searches the spirit of a man; it searches out his inmost being" (Proverbs 20:27). This is the original context for the proverbial "light going on" inside a man. It's *awareness of the fight.*

The Bible always affirms your conscience. When you surrender to God, your conscience is redeemed. And though God continually affirms it, Satan seeks to remold it. The flesh also tries to drown it. The Holy Spirit guides and shapes it, but the world minimizes its influence so your appetites and individual "rights" can have their way. The conscience is redeemed in a man who's surrendered to God. And know this: your conscience can be injured by not correctly responding to it in a timely manner. Habit kills. The Holy Spirit will always validate and urge you to make good on your conscience's warnings, prompting you to go back, and not put it off: "The Spirit explicitly says that in later times some will fall away from the faith, paying attention to deceitful spirits and doctrines of demons, by means of the hypocrisy of liars seared in their own conscience as with a branding iron" (1 Timothy 4:1–2, NASB). Get that? The dumbing down of conscience is an intentional strategy of evil. When we ignore the Holy Spirit's prompting, we desensitize our weapon.

Appropriate and Cooperate with the Holy Spirit Daily

When I travel, I never rent a car without a global positioning system. I don't want to waste time with maps. I want to get there. There's only one step: I have to *turn it on.* The system can be there, but if I'm not using it and following the instructions, I'm not going anywhere. Get the picture? Simple.

And yet when it comes to our relationship with the Holy Spirit, somehow we make it hard. The Bible says to do only two things when it comes to the Holy Spirit: appropriate and cooperate. We appropriate His leadership, influence, and control daily by simply placing ourselves under His control. It doesn't matter whether you're a pastor or a brand-new believer. All of us must practice this daily discipline to win against evil. We "turn on" what's already inside by saying, *Holy Spirit, I surrender to Your control today. Lead me, guide me, and control me.* Like I said, simple, but it's also *hard* because Satan viciously opposes our submission to that leadership. It's a *power* issue: "I pray that out of his glorious riches he may strengthen you with power through his Spirit in your inner being" (Ephesians 3:16).

We *activate* the system by praying that *right now.* Then, we must *cooperate* with where the Holy Spirit says to go in our actions and attitudes. That's the interactive part: "Pray in the Spirit on all occasions with all kinds of prayers and requests. With this in mind, be alert and always keep on praying for all the saints" (Ephesians 6:18). This passage is a battlefield scenario calling for close communication. Jesus told His disciples that the Holy Spirit would be His GPS residing in them to guide them in the fight.

In a war, the first thing an enemy will try to do is knock out your ability to communicate. But God's man discerns the Holy Spirit's voice very simply: it's always consistent with the character of God and His Word. We simply ask, "Does that align with the character of Christ and His Word?" If yes, that's the Holy Spirit. If no, it's not. This is fighting in its most basic form. The Holy Spirit will always give you a "fever" if an action or attitude plays into evil. He will make you pause and feel conflicted about certain decisions that may impact your relationships with

God and people. But through regularly appropriating and cooperating with the Spirit, God's man gets good at listening to the pause and develops a righteous "gut feeling," a discernment that becomes acute. This is his tactical advantage thanks to his *Holy Spirit Communication System* (HScom).

I've seen God's mighty weapons work powerfully in my life, and I hate to think how these weapons are gathering dust in many men's lives due to ignorance and incompetence. By default, we're giving Satan permission to prosecute his campaign. *No más!* Enough is enough. We must become masters at confronting and dealing with evil.

In the next chapter we continue the tour of our arsenal with some surprises and new challenges to "train up." Make no mistake, we're going after *functional* understanding of each weapon—not *intellectual.* One is good for battle, the other is good for nothing.

Remember, soldier, every effort you make to integrate and use God's weapons in your life counters evil. More important, it causes Satan and his agents to retreat, redeploy, and rethink their game plans. That's the way we like it. Instead of God's man retreating, we can have a new strategy: put evil on the run. Sounds better, doesn't it? *That's* what happens when we decide to use these weapons.

Result: those prison doors will just keep flying wide open.

armed and extremely dangerous: part two

Qui desiderat pacem, praeparet bellum.
From the Latin: "Let him who desires peace, prepare for war."
—FLAVIUS VEGETIUS RENATUS

In the book *Lone Survivor* we're introduced to a warrior of warriors:

> My name is Marcus. Marcus Luttrell. I am a United States Navy
> SEAL, Team Leader, SDV Team 1, Alfa Platoon. Like every
> other SEAL I am trained in weapons, demolition, and unarmed
> combat. I'm a sniper, and I'm the platoon medic. But most of
> all, I'm an American. And when the bell sounds, I will come
> out fighting for my country and for my teammates. If necessary,
> to the death. And that's not because the SEALs trained me to
> do so; it's because I'm willing to do so.... For me, defeat is
> unthinkable.[1]

Marcus is an elite sheepdog who cares deeply about protecting the sheep. His confidence is scary and very real. And if you care to know how a man can be so supremely self-assured without being cocky, you must pick up this book. From the first line, you can feel it oozing out of him, and you know this is true. Marcus knows who he is and what he's capable of when fully deployed in his identity and responsibility. And he's been equipped with the weapons and training.

You could say he's *intimate* with his gear. As you read his story of survival and battle in the mountains of the Hindu Kush, you know why he survives and the enemy dies in droves. Or in Marcus's own words: "No one can shoot like us." It's that combination of training, identity, healthy pride, and skill in the fight that makes you love this guy and, at the same time, strikes fear into the hearts of those who would tangle with him.

He's not just good, he's *really good.* He has to be, or he can't call himself a SEAL.

Bad guys, beware.

Fit to Fight

One of the main goals of this discussion is to deepen our sensitivity to one profound fact: weapons are only as good as our training. By now, I sense you feel in your gut, like I do, this inherent responsibility to train with your weapons—to train up, load up, suit up, and show up. And yes, I think we can safely say it's *a kindred spirit with the Lord Jesus Christ* moving inside. It's a spiritual reality, a brotherhood born of battle and blood, steeped in a proud tradition, and forged from one Man's willingness to lay down His life for us.

We can't explain this connection fully, but what we do know is this: every God's man gets Jesus *as a man*. This means you long to fight the way Jesus fought, to sacrifice the way He sacrificed, and to win liberation for someone else the way He liberated you. "In bringing many sons to glory, it was fitting that God, for whom and through whom everything exists, should make the author of their salvation perfect through suffering. Both the one who makes men holy and those who are made holy are of the same family. *So Jesus is not ashamed to call them brothers*" (Hebrews 2:10–11).

Women can appreciate this sentiment, even applaud it. But they can't sense the male bonding and our shared responsibility as men. It is the stuff of *brothers*. And that's why, as fighting God's men, we *live* the language of weapons, demolitions, and one-on-one struggles with our enemy. Not because we're armchair navy SEALs, but because all of these concepts are in the training manual. We are identity- and duty-bound to be proficient with them in all forms. Or else.

Or else what? Or else you can't call yourself a God's man.

God's Word

Roman soldiers exercised and trained heavily with the sword. More specifically, they were trained to thrust the sword versus cut with it. In fact, they made fun of those who preferred the cut to the thrust, and they relished a battle of styles. Roman strategist Flavius Vegetius Renatus explains the reason why:

> For the Romans not only made a jest of those who fought with
> the edge of that weapon, but always found them an easy conquest.
> A stroke with the edges, though made with ever so much force,

seldom kills, as the vital parts of the body are defended both by the bones and armor. On the contrary, a stab, though it penetrates but two inches, is generally fatal.... This was the method of fighting principally used by the Romans, and their reason for exercising recruits with arms of such a weight at first was, that when they came to carry the common ones so much lighter, the greater difference might enable them to act with greater security and alacrity in time of action.[2]

The sword was the Roman soldier's primary offensive weapon. He trained with it more than any other and learned how to wield it *lethally*. A *thrust* accomplished the job, where cutting gave the enemy a second chance. The author of Hebrews shows that he also was intimate with a sword and how the sword of God's man is best wielded in battle: "The word of God is living and active. *Sharper than* any double-edged sword, it *penetrates* even to dividing soul and spirit, joints and marrow; it *judges* the thoughts and attitudes of the heart" (Hebrews 4:12).

> *"On the contrary, a stab, though it penetrates but two inches, is generally fatal."*

There's a compare and contrast going on here between only grazing evil and killing it with a deep penetration of the Word into the heart. More profoundly, the end result of a strong thrust of God's Word is a *judgment*. *That* is what God's man is after in his fights with deception, temptation, and accusation on a personal level. And *that* is what he's after in a direct confrontation with evil.

A Roman soldier would move to parry a blow with his shield, create space, and then step and thrust his sword strategically into the flesh of his enemy. Similarly, God's man defends himself by moving into a blow with the shield of his faith, positioning the sword of God's Word, and thrust-ing it into the heart of evil. We witnessed this approach taken by Jesus in Luke 4. He parried Satan's blow by referencing Scripture, saying, "It is written," to counter the blow Satan levied at Him, and followed with, "Worship the Lord your God and serve him only." Each response was a strong, spoken, and deadly accurate thrust into the heart of the Tempter. The pattern of this dance to the death followed a rhythm: temptation, parry, thrust, temptation, parry, thrust, and so on. In the end, one Man stood alone.

The heart of God's man is one huge scabbard loaded with the Word of God. His tongue represents the sure and confident grip of a strong hand on the hilt, ready to unsheathe it at a moment's notice and thrust it into any situation warring against him, his faith, and his commitment to God's purposes. This is our culture as God's men and men of spiritual war. We make sure we are locked and loaded, full of the Word.

Witness our brotherhood of the blade, Job and Eliphaz of the Old Testa-ment, making sure the other is ready to parry and strike: "Accept instruc-tion from his mouth and lay up his words in your heart," says Eliphaz to Job. To which Job replies, "I have not departed from the commands of his lips; I have treasured the words of his mouth more than my daily bread" (Job 22:22; 23:12). It's a picture of the priority and proximity of the Word of God to a soldier of God. Just a like a SEAL's best friend in a fight is his rifle, the best companion of a God's man in a fight is the Word of God. We cannot live without it, and we cannot fight without it.

In our contest against evil, Satan tries to get us sloppy with our sword by manipulating or twisting the Scripture to fit his objectives. It's subtle but effective disinformation the Bible calls "doctrines of demons" (1 Timothy 4:1, NASB). You know a man is swallowing this stuff when on key issues of faith he's holding unbiblical views based on feelings, opinions, or personal agendas. These views may appear credible at first, but they're doomed to sabotage the man who holds them.

In these cases, it's a flip-flop: the Word of God is usurped by the opinions of man. When the Word of God ceases to be our absolute authority, Satan can mess with us and say, "Well, God really didn't mean that." You know you're encountering an evil doctrine masquerading as a biblical doctrine when it serves man's interests or pride. It might even smell *religious*. Watch out for these frauds, "For such men are false apostles, deceitful workmen, masquerading as apostles of Christ. And no wonder, for Satan himself masquerades as an angel of light. It is not surprising, then, if his servants masquerade as servants of righteousness. Their end will be what their actions deserve" (2 Corinthians 11:13–15). Just remind yourself it's evil behind the mask.

The sword of God's Word in hands carrying a strong sense of identity in Christ, aware of their authority in Christ, and intent on the Holy Spirit are more than fit to fight evil. "The mouth of the righteous man utters wisdom, and his tongue speaks what is just. The law of his God is in his heart; his feet do not slip" (Psalm 37:30–31).

Know your weapon intimately. Be ready to unsheathe it. And don't just graze—thrust.

Truth

There are two forces alone that shape and influence the hearts of men: *truth* and *lies*. Whatever wins that battle for a man's heart wins the battle for his character. The character of a man drives his conduct, shaping his blast zone of influence. That conduct will create health and life or sickness and death for those around him.

That's why we see Jesus defining Himself as *truth* and *life*. Satan is Jesus' exact opposite: "the father of lies" (John 8:44) and the one "who holds the power of death" (Hebrews 2:14). And man is caught in the cross fire.

The more we live in the truth, the more freedom we experience with God and people. The more we swallow the lies, the more slavery we experience in our flesh. This is why Jesus put in to His Father a special request for us before leaving Earth. Praying for His present and future disciples, He asked God to "make them holy—consecrated—with the truth" (John 17:17, MSG). Why did He pray this? He knew that in the end, a strong relationship with truth on the part of His men would mean an equally adversarial relationship with evil and the Devil.

The battle to be a man of truth is a battle fought on many fronts. He is

- able to be honest with God
- able to be honest with himself
- able to be honest with others
- teachable in the face of uncomfortable truth
- good with reality, not afraid of it
- good at meeting the demands of reality and changing accordingly
- desiring to use truth as a compass for decision making
- marinating in God's truth in the Bible
- proactively applying truth when it's discovered
- seeking out people of truth to keep him accountable
- taking responsibility

In the Scripture, the picture of truth is of a belt that holds together all other fittings of a warrior's clothing. It's the first thing that goes on: "Stand firm then, with the belt of truth buckled around your waist" (Ephesians 6:14). It is central to the fight. In the end, every encounter you'll have with evil is a *truth encounter.* Truth will confront the lie as good confronts evil, as the Holy Spirit confronts the flesh, and as God's Word confronts the world's values. All of these are truth encounters. Just as the Axis and the Allies fought bitterly and without rest at El Alamein, Normandy, and Stalingrad, so it is with the forces of righteousness and the forces of darkness in the battle for truth. A lot of resources are put there.

Why? Simple: truth always turns the tide against evil because truth exposes evil. Living in the truth liberates from evil, and speaking the truth defeats evil.

Think about it in your own life. Truth is what *is,* not what fits your feelings. Truth is the way things *are,* not the way you wish things were. Truth is the way God says things are; everything else is an opinion. It's what the bright light shows the situation to be, not what the darkness tries to pawn off. Truth is where the buck stops for evil: "This is the verdict: Light has come into the world, but men loved darkness instead of light because their deeds were evil. Everyone who does evil hates the light, and will not come into the light for fear that his deeds will be exposed. But whoever lives by the truth comes into the light, so that it may be seen plainly that what he has done has been done through God" (John 3:19–21).

fight fact
Being intimate with truth is synonymous with the ability to deal lethally with evil in all forms and at all levels.

God's man willingly puts himself in front of the light of truth. He has learned not to fear it because wise men know that all truth is God's truth.

The Blood

One time I asked my friend from the Middle East what blood represents to him, and he responded without hesitation, "Blood is life." In other words, blood is fundamental to existence; it is what procures and sustains life. It contains the whole story of creation, man, faith, and meaning all in one. Thus, blood is life.

God's man has an even deeper attachment to blood because faith in Christ brings him face to face with the blood of Christ. In short, no blood, no forgiveness. No forgiveness, no heaven. Theologians call this substitutionary atonement: His blood for your sin. I call it mind-blowing. The blood is what makes for our instant fellowship with other Christians and our common sense of gratitude to God. We are in the deepest possible debt to God for the blood of His Son on our behalf. That's why we cry and sing the old hymn at the same time: "What can wash away my sins? Nothing but the blood of Jesus."

Similarly, although I wouldn't call this a fellowship, guess what you and Satan have most in common? *The blood.* But that's where the common ground stops, because you could not have a more inverse relationship to anything than you have here. Satan was defeated by the blood; you were cleansed by it. Satan was betrayed by it; you were rescued by it. Satan was humiliated by it; you were exalted by your trust in it. The mention of the blood is repellent to him. That's why the Scripture says that what secured our initial victory over Satan on the cross is a *weapon* to secure our ongoing victory over him as believers.

Let's study film: "Now have come the salvation and the power and the kingdom of our God, and the authority of his Christ. For the accuser of our brothers, who accuses them before our God day and night, has been hurled down. They overcame him by the blood of the Lamb and by the word of their testimony; they did not love their lives so much as to shrink from death" (Revelation 12:10–11). For Satan, the blood is synonymous with the sacrificial death of Christ. It triggers his nightmares. Jesus snatched the victory from Satan when he believed he had Jesus' certain defeat. It's a Hall of Fame moment for Christ, a Hall of Shame moment for Satan. He whiffed with bases loaded in the bottom of the ninth and two outs in game seven of the World Series. Think he'd remember that? Think he'd want to be around anyone who mentions it?

So, God's man, that's your cue. Sing it. Pray it. Declare it. Remember it through deep communion. Do what you must do to remind the Great Loser of why he lost: that's right, *the blood.* Tell him now:

> Oh! precious is the flow
> That makes me white as snow;
> No other fount I know,
> Nothing but the blood of Jesus.

He won't hang around you anymore. This is the language he understands. Give it to him straight.

Prayer

When my brother committed suicide, I was a mess. For a lot of reasons. The circumstances surrounding his death and the revelations that later came out were devastating. He'd hurt many people, friends I knew and neighbors I had grown up with. On top of this, I was the one who had to attend to his *affairs* because he lived near me in Southern California.

It was a long week of horrific discovery about his past, the lives he'd ruined, and the irreversible impact of a life of crime. I found myself in a fog as I broke the coroner's seal on his apartment, saw on the table the alcohol and pills he'd used to kill himself, and began the process of sorting through all his earthly belongings. The cleanup, the trip to Northern California, seeing my devastated mother, and going through the difficult funeral left me depleted and worn out emotionally and physically. I was so spent that the night before I had to return to work, I was rocking myself like a baby, clutching my Bible to my chest and sobbing. Not my proudest moment. I knew I had to turn it over to God, but even that seemed hard.

In that moment, I mustered just enough energy to flop my Bible onto the coffee table, and when it fell open, I started to pray silently. *Oh God! Oh God! Please help me,* I thought. *I can't do this, I can't even move from this couch. Please help me, Father.*

Then, mysteriously, a sensation started making its way up my ankles and legs, peeling every ounce of stress and pressure away as it traveled to my head. God was answering my prayer in a way I'd never experienced before and perhaps never will again. The sensation kept ripping away the negative emotions inside as if someone was literally unloading my turmoil and replacing it with peace. It was tangible, palpable; it felt wonderful. All that power from my weak little effort to reach out and connect with God. It wasn't that my thoughts or words meant anything. It was where my feeble prayer was centered: in a *powerful* Person.

All *I* did was invite His participation.

Imagine Tiger Woods as your partner in a golf scramble, Warren Buffett as your financial backer for your business start-up, or a team of navy SEALs with you on a mission. All of these dudes possess some serious firepower, radically changing the odds of success and inspiring your own confidence. And while you may never experience these pairings, the Bible says that Jesus has your back and is ready and willing to war with you and for you—*if you just ask.* "I urge, then, first of all, that requests, prayers, intercession and thanksgiving be made for everyone—for kings and all those in authority, that we may live peaceful and quiet lives in all godliness and holiness. This is good, and pleases God our Savior, who wants all men to be saved and to come to a knowledge of the truth. For there is one God and *one mediator between God and men, the man Christ Jesus*" (1 Timothy 2:1–5).

In the words of Doc Holliday from the movie *Tombstone,* Jesus says, "I'm your huckleberry."

All prayer centered on Jesus Christ is powerful prayer.

Makes sense now, doesn't it, why prayer is one the most difficult disciplines to develop as God's man? Satan pulls out all the stops, engineers interruptions, rationalizations, and other diversions—anything to keep you from getting on your knees and connecting with the God of the universe. The difference between confronting a praying God's man and a prayerless one is like the difference between confronting a guy holding a squirt gun versus confronting Marcus Luttrell holding an

> *Prayer is fighting behavior.*

M60 machine gun. One guy can get you wet, and the other guy can fast-track a meeting with God.

Your decision to pray sends shivers through the world of evil because, once again, this is a language they *understand and fear* deeply. More to the point, they know who's going to show up on your behalf. Satan will suggest, "You can do that later." But the Bible says, "Pray continually" (1 Thessalonians 5:17). If you keep pounding the Enemy with heavy artillery, you'll confuse and disperse him. Not as a last resort but as your *very first option, every day, 24/7.*

The only thing I would add to that encouragement would be the word *dummy,* as in "Pray continually, dummy." Only a dummy would turn down the real-time support of God Himself in a toe-to-toe against evil. So we all need to stop moonlighting as morons and pray continually, dummy. Pray now. Pray in the morning, on the drive to work, before your next sales call, before your meetings, while driving home, on the plane for the person next to you, and every other chance you get. "And pray in the Spirit on all occasions with all kinds of prayers and requests. With this in mind, be alert and always keep on praying for all the saints" (Ephesians 6:18).

Prayer is fighting behavior.

Chemical Warfare

Do you know anyone with allergies? My wife and my friend Paul both have allergies. The funny thing about allergies is that they can turn symptomatic without warning. Invisible airborne agents make their way in and cause all sorts of reactions. What we see *physiologically* is a hyperactive response of the immune system to certain foreign invaders. The result is misery until medications kick in.

But here's a little secret: Satan has allergies. Spiritually speaking, there are behaviors that short-circuit his tactics and seriously irritate his system. More and more these days, I find that when I'm actively expressing the following character qualities in my life, the more protected I am against the Devil's tactics—and the more allergic to me he must feel. These are all strengthening disciplines for God's man and weakening influences for the Enemy.

Humility

This character quality is the antigen of pride and stimulates the production of spiritual antibodies: faith, surrender, and willing submission to God's will. So if you want to irritate the snot out of the Devil, stay humble before God and man. It's surprisingly not difficult if you remember who God is and who you are and the connection between you—a blood-streaked cross. Very humbling indeed.

Forgiveness

This behavior releases you from the grip of bitterness, resentment, and anger. It takes away a major fuel cell of satanic power in your life. God's man short-circuits many evils doing for others what Christ did for him. Unforgiveness is a foothold of Satan, giving him space on the beaches of your life. Forgiveness, offered freely and unconditionally, evicts the squatter and takes back the beach.

Gratitude

If you don't have an attitude of gratitude, then all you have is *attitude*. Apply liberal amounts of gratitude to your daily life because nothing else kills pride like gratitude. You will never meet a grateful narcissist. Gratitude is also an excellent disinfectant against envy, coveting, and discontentment. Gratitude is impartial: useful for both rich and poor. Satan knows that affluence without gratitude breeds discontentment. The more people have, the more apathetic they seem to become. Satan also knows that poverty without gratitude breeds envy—"If only I had their problems." Both envy and discontentment are angry requests for the same thing: autonomy. The message is, "I want out of my life!" This gets Satan salivating. The way to shut him down is to preempt those feelings by *being grateful*. It's a lifestyle, not an event. Gratitude replaces the hunger for autonomy with a settled submission to God's loving authority and sovereignty. That's called contentment.

Like me, you've probably got a lot of training to do to be a complete fighting man. I'm hit-and-miss on several of these disciplines at any given moment. The goal is to rearrange my life in such a way that using these weapons becomes a *lifestyle*. I want my life to be increasingly difficult for Satan to exploit. I want to know he's becoming more allergic to me each day. So take this advice: do a self-inventory, identify your deficiencies—whether in relationships or pride or whatever—and make your specific, daily, action-oriented plan to train up.

And I'm looking forward to that day when we'll all sit around in the great circle of brothers in heaven and trade stories. There will be plenty of time for stories later, I promise. I can't wait to hear them.

the ultimate weapon

I know what you can do. Your chief weapon is killing, but let me tell you what my chief weapon is. My chief weapon is dying. And I want to warn you that if you use yours, I will be forced to use mine.

—ROMANIAN PASTOR JOSEPH T'SON
to his persecutors

A final point: one weapon is primary in the fight with evil. Only one weapon has the greatest power over all others to kill evil.

In his book *Tools of War: The Weapons That Changed the World,* author Jeremy Black chronicles fifty weapons of war that altered history. When you read about the unlucky armies on the receiving end of these innovations, you can't help but feel pity for them. The tools Black selects have one common denominator: lopsided losses for the unlucky side who did not think of these new weapons first. The beauty of a great weapon is ultimately brutal for the other side.

The French experienced this reality at the Battle of Crécy on August 26, 1346, in northern France, which pitted the longbow of the English against the crossbow of the French. Never mind that the French outnumbered the English three to one. "Experienced archers could manage 8 to 10 arrows a minute. With this firing rate, the 5,000 English archers on the field of battle that day could launch 40,000–50,000 arrows a minute, or 700 a second. French infantry and cavalry alike were decimated under the barrage of deadly missiles, and the Battle of Crécy was won for the loss of only 200 English soldiers, to nearly 10,000 French dead. The conquest of France beckoned."[1]

The lesson? The best tactics, energy, and numbers are *useless* against distance and accuracy. So simple and yet so completely stunning. The French didn't stand a chance.

But even more significant, the victory must have produced an incredible confidence for the English's next conquest. Do you see an important connection to our own fight here?

Simple and Stunning

In warfare, technology triumphs. Against evil, *our* overwhelming force is obedience.

Listen to Jesus tell His soon-to-be killers about His mission and His ultimate weapon: "I know my sheep and my sheep know me—just as the Father knows me and I know the Father—and I lay down my life for the sheep. I have other sheep that are not of this sheep pen. *I must bring them also.* They too will listen to my voice, and there shall be one flock and one shepherd. The reason my Father loves me is that I lay down my life—only to take it up again. No one takes it from me, but I lay it down of my own accord. I have authority to lay it down and authority to take it up again. This command I received from my Father" (John 10:14–18). In obedience, Jesus modeled how God's man *always risks obedience toward his greatest hope.*

The power of obedience over evil is overwhelming to evil when you are willing to sacrifice for your greatest hope in Christ. Jesus' deep desire was simply to bring people into relationship with God. That strong hope created an even stronger willingness to obey and fight: "I lay down my life.... I lay it down of my own accord." The result: the hope of God's man fuels his *obedience* in the fight.

> *"No one takes it from me, but I lay it down of my own accord."*

The God-Man modeled how a strong eternal hope manifests in consistently strong choices. A weak hope manifests in weak choices. Obedience overwhelms evil, but the hope that drives obedience leads to victory. Jesus remembered what He was fighting for, and it wasn't simply to take Satan out to the shed for a good spanking. It was because of *you.* Your future with God was the strong hope that fueled a stronger, evil-killing obedience. And because of this, evil simply could not compete with the hopeful obedience of the God-Man. Think about that, God's man: a future inhabited by *you* fueled Jesus' overwhelming obedience and defeated all attempts by evil to get Him to compromise in His quest.

Don't miss it: high-octane, evil-defeating obedience has both personal and eternal results. Hope in your future with God fuels your fullest obedience to Him. The end result: evil can't compete, even as it couldn't compete with Christ.

Uneasiness Is the Compass

There's a shocking little discovery in the story of Jesus going to meet His destiny on Calvary. After wrestling with God over the agony before Him, releasing Himself to God's will, and coming back to His disciples only to find them asleep and unaware, Jesus said, "Rise, let us go! Here comes my betrayer!" (Matthew 26:46). What I want to point out is that instead of running away, Jesus deliberately and resolutely moved *toward* the evil, this great source of His personal and spiritual discomfort in prayer with God. Why? Because He's obedient to God.

fight fact
*Evil-defeating obedience
is synonymous with
discomfort for Christ.*

Where Christ felt discomfort in His soul and person, He moved forward to defeat the evil. Uneasiness was His compass.

My uneasiest, most uncomfortable moments with evil happen about the evil in my own heart. In fact, my biggest wins against evil have not been in the mission field but in the killing fields of my character—the places in me that sabotage Christlikeness and undermine my relationships with people, beginning most crucially with my wife. I call these the "see to it" areas: "See to it, then, that the light within you is not darkness" (Luke 11:35). These words of Jesus are burned on my brain mainly because they strongly indicate that God's man can *fake it.* Evil has a field day with men who do.

Just to lead out and demonstrate the importance of this, I'll share some of the "see to it" strongholds in my own life:

- surrendering my finances
- disciplining and saying no to myself for higher purposes

- confessing and confronting sexual temptation in open and accountable ways with my wife and other men
- addressing blind spots of pride
- having no secrets
- handling conflict and anger
- accepting that my identity as a man had suffered damage in my family of origin and was ripping at my marriage
- agreeing to see a counselor to defeat emotions that kept me bound to my past
- saying no to commitments to say yes to walking closer with God and strengthening relationships with people

These are just a few, but they should convince you my motives have been mixed up and the Enemy was given access. This is *my* stuff, and I'm not at all eager to admit my foibles. But I'm also acutely aware of the necessity of admitting and dealing with them and what that means for my personal fight with evil. Confronting these faults produced great *discomfort and anxiety* every time, and all required hope-filled and Satan-defeating obedience. Combined, these add up to many seasons of emotional discomfort, turmoil, and wrestling with forces of evil in my life.

> *I had to pick a fight with evil through simple obedience in the direction of my specific discomforts.*

But I stand before God and man today, able to testify to the power that eternal hope gives me to risk obedience, win freedom, and defeat Satan in each of these areas. In all of them, I had to first *recognize* that evil played a part in my struggle for light and Christlikeness. Second, I had to pick a fight with evil through simple obedience in the direction of my specific discomforts. While these are some of the biggies, there are also my daily skirmishes with evil that call for obedience:

- scanning the sports page rather than spending time in the Bible
- being grateful for my circumstances versus giving in to grumbling
- pausing before responding to a criticism
- expressing the discipline to say no to too many "opportunities"
- choosing forgiveness over resentment
- opening conversations with people about Jesus when prompted by the Spirit
- depending on God throughout my day instead of being self-sufficient
- not playing to people to please them or be accepted
- taking *full* responsibility when I blow it versus trying to defend myself

The Devil is definitely in the details of my obedience, and I want to stick it to him every chance I get. Why? Only to please God.

As You Will

Hope-filled obedience is a weapon for which the Devil has no answer and no solution. He was disarmed by it. He was disposed of by it. He was ultimately judged and his fate determined by it. He could not possess it or counter it, mitigate it, or defend against it. He couldn't detect it, deflect it, or destroy it. It was straightforward and striking, plain and powerful. Jesus Christ defeated evil, in the end, without a word of rebuke—just obedience.

There was no Scripture unplugged and unleashed. There was no sound or signal to record. There was no confrontation of the Spirit. There was no utterance of the truth, outing of the lie, or covering by the blood. There was no drama of the cross. Satan was overwhelmed, overcome, and overpowered by three words uttered, not on the cross, but in the Garden of Gethsemane: "As *you* will" (Matthew 26:39). The result of Christ's choice to follow God's lead was a thermonuclear disaster for the Devil. "Just as through the *disobedience of the one man the many were made sinners,* so also through the *obedience of the one man* the many will be made righteous" (Romans 5:19).

Your first and most effective weapon is personal obedience to God through the character of Christ. With it, you are never out of any fight against evil. But without it, all the fundamental skills we have discussed here are absolutely *powerless.*

To that end, we *must* make Christlikeness our supreme goal. From there, we appropriate more of His obedient character for more spiritual victories over evil and add more tactical weapons to our arsenal. We understand that God is more concerned that His Son's character comes forth in us than in the defeat of evil through us, because He deeply cares for our well-being. And in fact, our godly character ensures evil's defeat. This is the reason I wrote *Dream* before *Fight*—because Christlikeness in you creates a nightmare for Satan and all forms of evil trying to attack you.

When the Devil internalizes that his ploys and temptations are backfiring and forcing you to take on more of Christ's character by drawing you closer to Him through obedience, he will withdraw. Why? Because he's encountered a stronghold of Christ's presence instead of a stronghold he can exploit. Being fully saturated with Christ's living presence and fully willing to obey God's will is the ultimate weapon against evil.

It is so simple, so stunning, so beautiful, and so devastating to evil. This is our confidence for every fight we ultimately face. And there will always be another fight. The Bible says to count on it: "In fact, everyone who wants to live a godly life in Christ Jesus will be persecuted" (2 Timothy 3:12). God's plan for you is not immunity from the struggle but victory *in* the struggle. The eternal hope and drive of God's man pulls from him uncommon commitment that allows him to pray the same powerful words as his Leader: "As *You* will."

Saying "as *You* will" to God says the converse to Satan, the world, and the flesh: *"Not* as you will." Pray it right now, and send the Devil packing. Pray as Jesus prayed, that you may fight as He fought and live as He lived.

Launch this prayer of obedience again and again, and see how it prevails against overwhelming odds. You *will* prevail precisely because you possess the ultimate weapon. And you will take confidence in all your future battles, advancing against evil in incredible ways. Your obedience to God will develop both your sensitivity and acuity to evil, making you more fully aware, more fully equipped, and more fully engaged to take evil down wherever you encounter it.

Obedience to God allows you to live out the victory you've *already won* in Christ and to live more fully established in His authority. Remember, the true work of fighting evil is the work only a true God's man can do. "I felt I had to write and urge you to *contend for the faith* that was once for all *entrusted to the saints"* (Jude 3).

Only a saint is fit to pick a fight with evil. And you are a saint already, a title that's neither earned nor deserved. It's a matter of ownership. Believe in Christ's ownership over you, and you will be victorious.

The battle has fallen to us, my friend. Go charge that hill. Heaven beckons.

notes

Chapter 1

1. Counterterrorism center training handbook mission statement, name and location of center omitted for safety.
2. Gen. Douglas MacArthur, telegram to William Allen White, September 15, 1940, General Douglas MacArthur Memorial, MacArthur Square, Norfolk, VA.

Chapter 3

1. Jon E. Lewis, ed., *The Mammoth Book of True War Stories* (New York: Carrol & Graf, 1999), 272–73.
2. Cathleen Falsani, *The God Factor: Inside the Spiritual Lives of Public People* (New York: Farrar, Straus and Giroux, 2006), 12.

Chapter 4

1. CNN.com, "Vick Pleads Guilty, Apologizes," August 29, 2007, www.cnn.com/2007/US/law/08/27/michael.vick/index.html.

Chapter 6

1. Joseph Wambaugh, *Fire Lover: A True Story* (New York: Avon Books, 2003), 121.

Chapter 7

1. Joseph Wambaugh, interview by Soledad O'Brien, "Hunt for Serial Arsonist in DC Area," *American Morning,* CNN, July 8, 2003.
2. United States Census Bureau statistics taken from www.fathers.com, www.fathers.com/content/index.php?option=com_content&task =view&id=391. See also fathermag.com/news/2778-stats-shtml.

3. E. M. Bounds, *Winning the Invisible War* (Springdale, PA: Whitaker House, 1984), 11–12.

Chapter 8

1. John Cloud, "Atta's Odyssey," September 30, 2001, www.time .com/time/magazine/article/0,9171,1101011008-176917,00 .html.
2. Cloud, "Atta's Odyssey."

Chapter 9

1. *NBC Nightly News* with Brian Williams, October 22, 2007.
2. E. M. Bounds, *Winning the Invisible War* (Springdale, PA: Whitaker House, 1984), 92.

Chapter 10

1. Andrew Lycett, "Breaking Germany's Enigma Code," published on BBC History, August 1, 2001, and available online at www.bbc.co .uk/history/worldwars/wwtwo/enigma_01.shtml.
2. Oswald Chambers, *My Utmost for His Highest*, September 17.

Chapter 11

1. Pamela Gaudette, Bob Alexander, and Chris Branch, "Children, Sex and Violence: Calgary's Response to Child Prostitution," Child Welfare League of Canada, Fall 1996, www.cfc-efc.ca/docs/cwlc/ 00000826.htm.

Chapter 12

1. Thomas Sancton, "Anatomy of a Hijack," January 9, 1995, www.time.com/time/magazine/article/0,9171,982288,00 .html.

Chapter 13

1. Eric M. Jones and Ken Glover, eds., *Apollo Lunar Surface Journal,* 1995. At www.hq.nasa.gov/alsj/frame.html, click "Apollo 13" in the "Main Menu" frame, then click "Mission Summary" in the "Apollo 13 Sub-Menu" frame.

2. Cathleen Falsani, *The God Factor: Inside the Spiritual Lives of Public People* (New York: Farrar, Straus and Giroux, 2006), 11.

Chapter 14

1. Adapted with permission from Dave Grossman and Loren W. Christensen, *On Combat* (Jonesboro, AR: PPCT Research Publications, 2004).

Chapter 17

1. Marcus Luttrell, *Lone Survivor: The Eyewitness Account of Operation Redwing and the Lost Heroes of SEAL Team 10* (New York: Little, Brown, 2007), 6–7.

2. Flavius Vegetius Renatus, *The Military Institutions of the Romans (De Re Militari),* trans. John Clarke (1767), www.pvv.ntnu.no/~madsb/home/war/vegetius/dere03.php#00.

Chapter 18

1. Jeremy Black, *Tools of War: The Weapons That Changed the World* (London: Quercus, 2007), back cover.

about the author

Kenny Luck is the men's pastor at Saddleback Church in Lake Forest, California, where more than seven thousand men are connected in small groups. He is also the founder and president of Every Man Ministries, which helps churches worldwide develop and grow healthy men's communities.

He is an ECPA Platinum Award–winning author who has authored and coauthored more than eighteen books, including *Dream*; *Risk*; *Every Man, God's Man*; *Every Young Man, God's Man;* and the Every Man Bible Studies from the best-selling Every Man Series published by WaterBrook Press/Random House. Kenny has made numerous radio and television appearances as an expert on men's issues including ABC Family, Christian Broadcasting Network, and more than one hundred other radio and television programs worldwide. He has been a featured contributor to Rick Warren's *Ministry Toolbox, New Man Magazine, Men of Integrity, The Journal,* and *Young Believer* magazine.

Kenny is a graduate of UCLA, where he met his wife, Chrissy. They have three children, Cara, Ryan, and Jenna, and live in Trabuco Canyon, California.

For more information, contact:
Every Man Ministries
(949) 766-7830
www.everymanministries.com